The Gospel of Nonduality

A Spiritual Interpretation of the Gospel of John

MARSHALL DAVIS

Scripture quotations are from the (NASB®)
New American Standard Bible®, Copyright ©
1960, 1971, 1977, 1995, 2020 by The
Lockman Foundation. Used by permission.
All rights reserved..

ISBN: 9798594933729

CONTENTS

PREFACE

This book began as a series of talks for my podcast, *The Tao of Christ*, which were also aired on my YouTube channel, *Christian Nonduality*. At the beginning of the coronavirus pandemic in early 2020, I started the podcast as a platform to share some of my books in audio format. Later I began to write new material on the subject of Christian nonduality.

Many of these online talks used biblical texts and interpreted them as expressions of nonduality. Some listeners asked if I had ever considered going through the entire Bible, interpreting it as nonduality. Such a monumental task would take a lifetime to finish, but I agreed to go through one book. There are several books in the Bible I could have chosen. I considered Genesis, Job and Ecclesiastes, but I opted to do a Christian text.

There are a number of ancient non-canonical Christian gospels that are nondual in character, most notably in the Hag Hammadi Library. They are often called "gnostic" as a way to discredit them, but they are authentically Christian. I did one episode on the Gospel of Thomas as a test project, and it became the most listened-to episode on my podcast.

The only canonical Christian writing that has nonduality as its central theme is the Gospel of John. I remembered studying in college and seminary about the Gnostic influence on John, but I was unprepared for just how thoroughly the Gospel of John embraces nonduality. It is not an exaggeration to call it "the gospel of nonduality," hence the title of this volume.

This book is intended for both Christians and those who would consider themselves "spiritual but not religious." It is for those who sense something more in Christianity than the moralistic and doctrinal religion it has become. The gospel of Jesus Christ is at heart experiential. I call it mystical, in the sense that it is more than an emotional or personal experience. It testifies to a direct awareness of the Divine and our essential unity with all that exists.

Anyone who has "tasted the heavenly gift" of the nondual Kingdom of God is not satisfied with the intellectual or ethical approach of traditional Christianity. This book is for them. The vast majority of my readers and listeners have become disenchanted with orthodox Christianity, but have not given up on the message of Christ. This book is for you.

Marshall Davis
Baptism of the Lord, January 2021

A GOSPEL OF NONDUALITY

Jesus of Nazareth preached a gospel of nonduality. You would not know that by listening to most Christian preachers today. But if one looks carefully, the original nondual message of Christ can be found in the New Testament. This is not a matter of reading one's own spiritual perspective into the text. This is a matter of sifting the nondual wheat from the dualistic chaff. This nondual message is most clearly proclaimed in the Gospel of John.

The Gospel of John is considered by biblical scholars to be the latest of the four gospels, yet it is the only book in the Bible with a direct connection to one of the original twelve apostles of Jesus. It is the only Gospel based on the firsthand testimony of someone who heard Jesus teach. The other three were written by people who neither knew Jesus nor heard him teach.

The Gospels of Mark and Luke do not even pretend to be firsthand accounts of the life and teachings of Jesus. Neither Mark nor Luke were apostles. These second-generation Christians were traveling companions of the apostle Paul, who himself never met Jesus or heard him preach. Furthermore the names of Mark and Luke were attached to these gospels in the second century – one hundred years after Jesus' death. We have no reason to think these are accurate. If anything they are testimony to the fact that in the second century the church leaders knew these Gospels were not written by apostles.

The Gospel of Matthew does bear the name of a disciple of Jesus, who was also known as the tax collector Levi. His name also does not appear in connection to this gospel under one hundred years after the events it describes. There is no external or internal evidence to connect the gospel to this apostle. In fact there is internal evidence to the contrary. The Gospel of Matthew copies most of the Gospel of Mark word for word. It would be strange for an eyewitness to the events to copy the account of a man who was not there.

Most importantly the Gospel of Matthew copies Mark's story of Jesus calling Matthew/Levi to be his disciple verbatim. It is unbelievable that the apostle Matthew would copy someone else's account of the most important day in his life. Why wouldn't he tell his story in his own words? Why would he copy and paste an account written by someone who was not there and never even met Jesus? It makes no sense at all. For that reason most biblical scholars believe that the apostle Matthew did not pen the gospel that bears his name.

Most of the rest of the New Testament books were written by the apostle Paul, who never met Jesus and seems unfamiliar with his teachings and ministry. Paul's message is nothing like the message that Jesus proclaimed. Christianity as we know it today is the creation of Paul more than Jesus or the twelve apostles. Paul turned the simple message of Jesus into a Gentile Roman religion.

Even the earliest Jerusalem Church – which was mostly likely to retain the original message of Jesus –

quickly fell under the influence of Jesus' brother
James, known as James the Just. James became the
leader of the church after Jesus' death. James was
not an apostle. He was not a disciple of Jesus. He did
not hear Jesus preach or believe in him during his
lifetime. But somehow, James wrestled control of the
new movement from Peter and the other apostles
after Jesus died. It probably had to do with the fact
he was his biological brother. Apparently blood is
thicker than baptismal water.

In this way earliest Christianity quickly moved
from being about the nondual message of Jesus to
being dominated by the dualistic message about
Jesus crafted by apostles like Paul and James and
those that followed them. This dualistic gospel is
expounded in almost all of the books included in our
New Testament. One of the exceptions is the Gospel
of John. For this reason I have chosen it as my text
in proclaiming the nondual gospel of Jesus.

I am not saying that the gospels of Matthew,
Mark, and Luke do not include authentic teachings
of Jesus. They certainly do. But the gospel writers
simply passed down the oral tradition they had
received second and third hand. The Gospel of John
is the only gospel that actually says that it is
connected to one of the original twelve apostles. This
was the apostle John, the son of Zebedee, the
brother of James (not to be confused with the other
James who was Jesus' brother.) John is called
throughout the gospel "the beloved disciple" or "the
disciple that Jesus loved" which shows the closeness
of John to Jesus.

We find John mentioned specifically in the final
verses of the gospel. Speaking of the Beloved Disciple
it says: "This is the disciple who testifies of these
things, and wrote these things; and we know that his
testimony is true. And there are also many other
things that Jesus did, which if they were written one

by one, I suppose that even the world itself could not contain the books that would be written. Amen."

These verses inform us that the Gospel of John is based on the writings of the apostle John. "This is the disciple who testifies of these things, and wrote these things." These verses also refer to a group of people identified as "we." "And we know that his testimony is true." This "we" is understood by biblical scholars to be the spiritual community that developed around the apostle John in the first century. Early church historians tell us the Johannine community was located in Ephesus in Asia Minor, modern day Turkey, and included Mary the mother of Jesus. It is out of this spiritual community, which included the two people closest to Jesus (John and Mary) that this Gospel of John came.

There is a third person mentioned in the text, who is the actual writer of the finished gospel (a "ghost writer" you would call him today) or at least the final editor of the book. He refers to himself as "I." He writes: "And there are also many other things that Jesus did, which if they were written one by one, I suppose that even the world itself could not contain the books that would be written." He refers to himself in the first person, but is someone different from John, who is always addressed in the third person. This "I" is presumably part of the "we," the spiritual community that grew up around the beloved disciple whom we know as John.

All this evidence indicates that the Gospel of John is the only one of the four gospels that can be tied to one of the twelve disciples, those who lived with Jesus and heard him teach. That makes this Gospel very important. Furthermore John was one of Jesus' closest disciples. At the Last Supper he is seated next to Jesus. John was leaning against Jesus, resting his head on Jesus's breast. That is a depiction of the intimate relationship Jesus had with John. They were close. The fact that John was seated next to Jesus also meant that he had high standing among the apostles. The other gospels confirm that Peter, James (the son of Zebedee, not Jesus' brother) and John, were an inner circle that Jesus would often teach privately.

For these reasons the Gospel of John can be expected to have the best insight into what Jesus actually taught. It captures the spirit of Jesus' teachings. It is also the most nondualistic of the four gospels. In this Gospel Jesus is a proclaimer of what he calls the Kingdom of God, Eternal Life or simply Life. I call it "unitive awareness" or "nondual awareness."

The Gospel of John is organized around seven teachings that Jesus gave, which speak of his true nature and identity. All of them begin with the words "I am," and are known as the I AM Sayings. 1) I AM the Bread of Life. 2) I AM the Light of the World. 3) I AM the door or gate. 4) I AM the Good Shepherd. 5) I AM the resurrection and the life. 6) I AM the way, the truth, and the life. 7) I AM the true vine.

These "I AM" statements are variations of the primary teaching of Jesus in Chapter 8 where he says: "Truly, truly, I say to you, before Abraham was, I AM." The phrase "I AM" is the central teaching of Jesus. It is hub around which the other seven "I AM" statements radiate like spokes on a wheel. When Jesus said "I AM," he was equating himself with God who declared himself to Moses to be "I AM" or "I AM THAT I AM." It is the meaning of the divine name YHWH. Jesus was identifying himself with the Divine. This nondual message is why Jesus was eventually executed by the religious authorities.

This "I AM" statement echoes throughout the Gospel of John. As I go through this Gospel I will bring us back to this statement over and over again.

This sense of identity with the Divine is the gospel of nonduality. It is the essence of all true religion. Jesus makes it clear in the Fourth Gospel that this awareness of the Divine is what he wants his followers to know. This is nondual awareness. This is the nondual message of the Gospel of John.

THE NONDUAL WORD

In this chapter I begin our study of the text of Gospel of John, interpreting it as a proclamation of the message of nonduality. The Gospel of John begins in the beginning. It reprises the famous words of Genesis 1 "In the beginning ...." But instead of telling a dualistic story of creation, "In the beginning God created the heavens and the earth..." it says "In the beginning was the Word...." Instead of telling a story it weaves a poem that describes how this present dualistic world came to be, and how it is in reality nondual. The Gospel begins:

"In the beginning was the Word, and the Word was with God, and the Word was God. The same was in the beginning with God. All things were made through Him, and without Him nothing was made that was made. In Him was life, and the life was the light of men. And the light shines in the darkness, and the darkness did not comprehend it."

"In the beginning was the Word." As the chapter continues it becomes clear that this "Word" that he is talking about is Christ. Not just the human named Jesus, but the Universal Christ who was at the beginning of the universe. Later in this gospel Jesus affirms this interpretation of his true nature, saying,

"Before Abraham was, I am."

The Word that was in the beginning was "I AM." The nondual truth at the heart of the Gospel of John is articulated in the words "I AM." This is the gospel. This "I AM" is what is meant in the gospel of John when it uses the word God. It says clearly here, "the Word was God." This statement is not only affirming the divinity of Christ, as traditional Christianity asserts. This Word affirms the identity of God. God is the Word "I AM," which in the Greek language is one word εἰμί (pronounced "eye me") and sometimes two words in order to emphasize the I: ἐγὼ εἰμί (pronounced "eggo eye me").

The Word from which the universe was formed, "through which all things were made," is this Word "I AM." If you had to sum up the message of Jesus in the Gospel of John it is "I AM." In Chinese spiritual tradition this original divine Word is known as the Tao. The oldest and still most popular Chinese translation of the New Testament translates the opening words of John's Gospel: "In the beginning was the Tao. And the Tao was with God and the Tao was God."

In Indian spiritual tradition this Divine Word is AUM, which is said to have originated as the sound of a breath. Similarly the word for breath in both Hebrew and Greek is the same as the word for Spirit. AUM is the Word chanted before a scriptural recitation in Hinduism, Buddhism, and Jainism. This syllable is found at the beginning and the end of chapters in the Vedas, the Upanishads, and other Hindu texts.

In the Torah the Divine word is YHWH (Yahweh) which is also said to be the sound of a breath. This word YHWH is said to be unpronounceable. To this day Jews will not speak the Divine Name while reading the Torah. This unpronounceable and unknowable Word means: "I am" or "I am that I am."

This is the eternal Word referred to at the beginning of the Gospel of John.

It is the primordial essential unity out of which the diversity of the universe emerged. It is nonduality out of which duality came without changing the essential unity. "In the beginning was the Word, and the Word was with God, and the Word was God. The same was in the beginning with God." Here it says that the Word was identical to God. It also says that the Word is with God. To be with God implies separation - duality. It means there is two.

Here is the emergence of two from One. Then there is the appearance of "all things" from the two. It says, "All things were made through Him (meaning the Word), and without Him nothing was made that was made." Most translations use the personal pronoun "Him" here, but in Greek the pronoun simply refers to the masculine word logos, word.

In English it is best translated, "All things were made through the Word, and without the Word, nothing was made that was made." The whole universe came from the One and the Two. This creation account reminds me of the Tao Te Ching, which says, "The Tao begot one. One begot two. Two begot three. And three begot the ten thousand things." The "ten thousand things" refers to the universe.

The Tao Te Ching says that the universe comes from the Three, which is reminiscent of the Christian concept of the Trinity. In Christian theology all three persons of the Trinity have a role in creating the universe. This shows how amazingly connected these spiritual traditions are. They are talking about the emergence of multiplicity from unity, duality from nonduality.

John then says, "In this Word was life, and the life was the light of humans. And the light shines in the darkness, and the darkness did not comprehend it."

When I read this passage, I think of scientific documentaries about the Big Bang that began the universe. Science says that originally there was one undifferentiated unity called the Singularity (which sounds a lot like nonduality), out of which came light and eventually life.

This word Life is used throughout the Gospel of John as shorthand for Eternal Life. The Gospel is not just talking about biological life coming about as a product of creation. There is a Greek word for that type of life if that is what he meant – bios. The word used here is zoe, which is spiritual life, eternal life, divine life. To know divine life is salvation in Christianity. In other spiritual traditions it is known as nirvana, moksha, enlightenment, awakening or liberation.

This is what the Gospel of John calls Life. It says that the Word is life. In other words "I AM" is eternal life. To know this "I AM" is life and this life is the light of humans. It is no accident that the word enlightenment includes the word light. To see all things by the light of "I AM" is enlightenment. It is eternal life.

"And the light shines in the darkness and the darkness did not comprehend it." This light of I AM shines in the darkness of the human condition. This creation poem of John Chapter One is so much more than a rehash of how the physical universe came into being. It is so much more than the unscientific creationism espoused by so many Christians today. This is talking about the spiritual condition of humanity. Humans are living in darkness. They do not see the light. They do not comprehend it. "And the light shines in the darkness, and the darkness did not comprehend it." Another word for this is ignorance. Not being able to see this light is to live in spiritual darkness and ignorance.

The solution to darkness is the light of I AM. True

life is to see the Light and walk by the light of the Word. That sentence is not talking about the Bible. So many Christians call the Bible the Word of God, and treat the Bible as a substitute for God. That is idolatry. It is called bibliolatry. The Bible never refers to itself as the Word of God! That is later religious invention. When the Bible talks about the Word it is talking about direct inspiration from God, not secondhand revelation transmitted through a book.

God is the Word. Christ is the Word. The most the Bible says about sacred writings is that certain books were inspired by God and useful. That is it. The concept of a book as the Word of God is a subtle way humans have of distancing themselves from God by placing a book between them and God, thereby avoiding direct awareness of God. That is bibliolatry and a formula for remaining stuck in duality. Unfortunately that is exactly where most of Christianity lives.

The prologue of John says the Word is God. The Word is I AM. This is the Word from which the universe was born. This Word is Life and this life is the light of humans. The light shines in the darkness, and the darkness does not comprehend it. To hear and recognize this Word is to wake up to Eternal life.

CHRISTIAN ENLIGHTENMENT

The Word that gave birth to the universe is the "I AM" or the Logos of Christian tradition. In the Hebrew tradition it is Yahweh or HaShem (meaning the Name). It is the AUM of the Indian tradition and the Tao of the Chinese tradition. The Gospel of John says that this Eternal Word "became flesh." Christianity understands this happening in Jesus. This is what makes this Christian nonduality. Every spiritual tradition articulates the Perennial Philosophy, as Aldous Huxley calls it, in its own vocabulary. The Gospel of John articulates it using Christian vocabulary. I am a Christian, so this is the vocabulary I use, but I try to draw parallels to other traditions whenever I can.

John 1:9-14 says that this Word - the Primordial and Eternal Christ - enlightens every human being. "The true light that enlightens every man was coming into the world." Another translation says, "The true light was that which enlightens everyone who comes into the world." In other words this is saying that everyone is enlightened! The Word was enlightening people long before the Word became flesh in Jesus.

What an extraordinary thing for this Christian apostle to say! This statement in John's Gospel is extraordinary in its universalism and inclusivism. It is also extraordinary in saying that spiritual enlightenment, which is sought after by so many spiritual pilgrims and seekers, is already reality for every person in the world. We are already enlightened or saved or liberated or awake or whatever term you want to use.

In actuality enlightenment actually does not happen to a "person." When enlightenment is recognized, it is seen that there is no person. Enlightenment is present, and the person ceases to be. There is just the Word "I AM." The Word is seen as expressed in and through this body-mind. That is incarnation. Christianity says that the True Light was incarnated - enfleshed, consciously bodily present -in the man known to history as Jesus of Nazareth. Yet this passage says that people did not recognize this.

"The true light that enlightens every man was coming into the world. He was in the world, and the world was made through him, yet the world knew him not. He came to his own, and his own received him not. But to all who received him, who believed in his name, he gave power to become children of God; who were born, not of blood nor of the will of the flesh nor of the will of man, but of God. And the Word became flesh and dwelt in us, full of grace and truth; we have beheld his glory, glory as of the only Son from the Father." John 1:9-14

John uses three different words for recognizing the True Light: knowing, receiving and believing. Life and Light – Enlightenment and Awakening – was present, but people did not know it. They did not receive it. They did not believe it. They were living in spiritual darkness and ignorance. It is the same today.

The Christian gospel says that Jesus is present here now but people do not see it. Christ is not dead and gone. Christ is alive. This is the meaning of the Resurrection and the Holy Spirit. "I am with you always," Jesus said after the Resurrection. The Eternal Christ is present now. The Kingdom of God is here now. Enlightenment is present here now. It is just a matter of knowing, receiving and believing.

"He was in the world, and the world was made through him, yet the world knew him not." To "know" in the Bible is not mental or intellectual knowledge. It is not holding right doctrines or reciting correct creeds. The verb "know" is used in the Bible for sexual intimacy. Knowing Christ is about spiritual intimacy with the divine. It is about becoming one with God, just as the Bible says that in sexual union two humans become one flesh. We become one with God. This is unitive knowledge or unitive awareness.

"He came to his own, and his own received him not. But to all who received him, who believed in his name, he gave power to become children of God." The word "receive" in Greek means "to join to one's self." It means to become one - like when people are joined in marriage or by blood. The difference is that when we are joined with Christ, the separate egos cease to be and there is only Christ. As Paul wrote: "It is no longer I who live but Christ who lives in me." Receiving Christ means selflessness – no self. To receive Christ means there is no longer an "I", which is the Greek words ego. There is only Christ.

The passage also talks about believing in his name. "But to all who received him, who believed in his name, he gave power to become children of God." This is not referring to the name Jesus. The name Jesus has not been mentioned yet in this Gospel. This is referring to the Eternal Christ that was before the man Jesus. This passage uses the phrase "the Word." One could paraphrase Jesus' words "Before Abraham was, I am" and say just as truthfully, "Before Jesus was, I am."

The name is "I AM." This is the Eternal Name, the Word, the Logos. This is the name that Moses learned at Mount Sinai in the burning bush. In that story in Exodus it is called the eternal name. "This is my name forever, the name you shall call me from generation to generation." The Unspeakable Eternal name is the Name that is to be received and believed.

"But to all who received him, who believed in his name, he gave power to become children of God; who were born, not of blood nor of the will of the flesh nor of the will of man, but of God." This is what it means to be "born again." It is difficult for those of us who have been part of Evangelicalism not to think of terms like "born again" and "receiving him" in evangelical terms. To be "born again" does not mean saying a little prayer and beginning a personal relationship with Jesus. Such language is never used in the Bible. It is not about having Jesus as your BFF.

Relationships are by nature dualistic. Jesus remains different and separate and apart from us. But the Gospel of John is talking about nondual identity. When you truly receive Jesus into your heart there is no room for you. There is only room enough for Jesus. The ego that wants to have a relationship must die for one to be born again. When one truly and completely receives Jesus, then there is only Jesus. And by Jesus I mean the Eternal Christ, the I AM.

Sometimes evangelicals say, "It is not a religion. It is a relationship." I say that it is not a religion or a relationship. It is resurrection. To be born again means to die and be resurrected to a new identity. It is to die to self and discover who we really are – our true identity. We die to who we thought we were and discover our true selves. One translation says this explicitly: "He made [them] to be their true selves, their child-of-God selves."

The gospel is not just about who Jesus is; it is about who we are. Not who we are physically – which is described as being born of blood or born of the flesh. It is not who we are socially – which is called the will of man. Our True Self is not our psychological self or the societal self. It is who we are spiritually as children of God.

It is not about us at all, but about who dwells in us: the Son of God. The final verse says, "And the Word became flesh and dwelt in us." Most translations render this as "among us," but it is better translated "in us" or "within us." The Greek word used is "en," from which we get the English word "in." It is the same word used when Jesus says that the Kingdom of God is "within us." The Word dwells in us. I AM is our true identity. It is no longer I who lives, but Christ who lives in me.

The Letter to the Colossians calls this "Christ in you, the hope of glory." John says, "The Word became flesh and dwelt in us, full of grace and truth; we have beheld his glory, glory as of the only Son from the Father." The Indwelling One is described as "full of grace and truth" and having "glory as of the only Son from the Father."

This is often translated as the "only begotten from the Father" or "the one and only Son." Christians have turned this into an exclusivistic claim, saying that Christians have a monopoly on God because we believe in the only begotten Son of God and those other religions do not! This is obviously not what it means here, for it says that this Word enlightens everyone who comes into the world. All enlightenment is of this One. There is only One and we all partake of this One. To say "one and only Son" is the same as saying there is only one God. Divine Reality is One. This One includes all. One is Nondual. By being joined to this One who enlightens every person, we partake of this One Reality that we call God. That is what it means to be children of God, born of God.

THE MAN WHO DID NOT WAKE UP

In this chapter we look at a person who is mentioned repeatedly in the first chapter of the Gospel of John: John the Baptist, not to be confused with John the apostle. I am calling him "the man who did not wake up." We could call him the unChrist or the unBuddha. When people came to John and asked who he was, he said clearly, "I am not the Christ." He was a popular preacher in his day and even considered a prophet by many people, including Jesus. But he never saw the Kingdom of God, which was Jesus' term for nondual awareness.

John the Baptist is described in the Gospel of Luke as a cousin of Jesus, just six months older than Jesus. He was a solitary prophet who lived, preached and baptized in the wilderness of Judea. It is possible that he was a hermit like the Desert Fathers of the third century. There is conjecture by some scholars that he was an Essene or at least connected to the Qumran Community near the Dead Sea, which is famous for preserving the Dead Sea Scrolls.

The gospels picture him as a charismatic figure, who wore a tunic made of camel's hair and ate a diet of honey and locusts. These "locusts," by the way, are the fruit of the locust tree known as carob. This tree has edible pods, the beans of which are used today as a chocolate substitute. John was not munching on grasshoppers, like so many readers assume. He was snacking on something more like cacao or cocoa beans.

In all the gospels John the Baptist is a transitional figure. He comes before Jesus and prepares the way for Jesus. He baptizes Jesus. He proclaims a message similar to that of Jesus, "Repent, for the Kingdom of God is at hand." He points people to Jesus, but does not become a disciple of Jesus. Near the end of his life he becomes uncertain about Jesus' identity. From prison he sent a disciple to Jesus asking him if he really was the Messiah or whether he should look for someone else.

John is the portrait of a spiritual seeker who never finds what he was looking for. In the gospels of Matthew and Luke, Jesus gives this assessment of John: "Truly I tell you, among those born of women there has risen no one greater than John the Baptist. Yet even the least in the kingdom of heaven is greater than he." According to Jesus, John never made into the Kingdom.

John the Baptist is like the spiritual seekers of today. He represents the spiritually minded person who has a lot of spiritual ideas and says all the right things, but has not known the spiritual reality of the Kingdom of God. That is why Jesus said, "the least in the kingdom of heaven is greater than he." John had not entered the Kingdom. He had not awakened to Reality.

He is like the seeker today who believes in enlightenment and desires it, but has not experienced it. Such people know all the right words and ideas. They have glimpsed the Kingdom from afar, enough to know it is real, but have not entered through the narrow gate. John had seen the Light but had not identified with the Light. The Gospel of John says of him: "There was a man sent from God, whose name was John. This man came for a witness, to bear witness of the Light, that all through him might believe. He was not that Light, but was sent to bear witness of that Light."

When John was asked if he is the Messiah, he admits he is not. So he was no imposter or charlatan; he was sincere. Then they ask, "Who are you?" John declares he is "a voice crying in the wilderness," quoting from Isaiah. That certainly describes a lot of people today. There are a lot of spiritual seekers wandering in the wilderness seeking for deliverance, liberation, salvation, awakening. They are thirsting for it like a person craving water in a desert.

John admits his spiritual condition. He said of Jesus, "I did not know him" even when he was baptizing him. John knew Jesus as his cousin. He even knew that Jesus was the "I AM" of Israel. John said of Jesus, "After me comes a Man who is preferred before me, for He was before me.'" This is a reference to Jesus' statement "Before Abraham was, I am." John called Jesus the Son of God. John knew about Christ, but it was knowing at a distance. Dualistic knowing.

Spiritual seekers today can be very knowledgeable. But like John they have not awakened to Reality. John seems to have died before he had that awakening. He was executed as a young man in his early thirties. Jesus and his cousin, who was the same age and probably shared a family resemblance, are examples of two spiritual paths. One man woke up and one did not. John was a seeker who never woke up. His life is a cautionary tale for seekers today.

John the Baptist is a transitional figure caught in duality but yearning for nonduality. For that reason he is a character that many people can identify with. He has something to say to those who have seen the Kingdom but not entered it. For unless one has a sudden and complete awakening, like Jesus did or like the Buddha did, we all are in transition.

Awakening is not a once-and-for-all event for most people. For some people it may be instantaneous and complete. But even Jesus took forty days in the wilderness to figure out what had happened to him at his awakening, which occurred at his baptism. Awakening involves a process of integrating the new reality into everyday consciousness. It is like a seed growing, which is why Jesus used that metaphor for the Kingdom of God so often in his parables. The seedling breaks through the ground to the Light in one moment, but that is just the beginning. Then it grows and matures and flowers. There is a process of opening up to Reality.

That process is our body and mind's adjustment to Reality. Nondual Reality is always here now. It does not change. But our temporal experience changes. In that way we all are in transition. If you have had a glimpse of the Kingdom, you are like a seed that has sprouted and broken through the surface of the Ground of Being into the Light.

That process has perils, which Jesus' parable of the Sower speaks about. There is no guarantee that the seed of the Kingdom will take root in our lives and flourish. I know that first hand. Once I glimpsed the Kingdom I pushed it away for twenty years, afraid of the consequences of the death of the self. The growing seed of the Kingdom needs to be nurtured. I wish I had someone to tell me that thirty years ago. It would have saved me a lot of suffering.

One thing John says is very helpful in this regard. In speaking to his disciples about the relationship between him and Christ in chapter 3 of the Gospel of John, he says of Christ, "He must increase; I must decrease." That sums up the process. The I - the self, the ego - must decrease and Christ must increase. Once Christ is glimpsed as our True Self, the process begins. In time Christ increases and we decrease, until there is no self and only Christ.

John is an example of a traditionally religious person, a devout Christian who knows there is something more to the spiritual life but has not found it yet. As the prologue says, John understood himself not as the Light but bearing witness to the Light. That is a good description of the traditional Christian path where the Beloved and the Lover are separate. Worship is an expression of such love. There is nothing wrong with this traditional worship of God. It gives the ego something to do.

I do not reject church worship or traditional Christianity. I love the church. I worship regularly in a traditional church. I preach occasionally in such churches, when they dare to let me into the pulpit! But there is more to the Christian life than this dualistic religious expression. Most Christians are like John the Baptist. They are a witnesses to the Light only. They have not been consumed by the Light until there only Light.

The traditional Christian pattern of worshipping and serving Christ is good, but it is not the best. In traditional Christianity there always remains a separation between the Christian and the Christ. In the Kingdom of God there is no separation. There is union in the "I AM" as "I AM. In the Kingdom of God, we are one with the Light of the world who is Jesus Christ. The spiritual life is a process of realizing that unity and identity.

THE PATH OF DIRECT INQUIRY

One day John the Baptist was with two of his disciples, and he saw Jesus walk by. He exclaimed, "Behold the Lamb of God!" I can imagine Jesus saying under his breath, "Give me a break, John. Will you stop saying these things?!" Anyway John's two disciples follow Jesus down the road. Jesus turns around and says, "What do you want?" They answer, "Rabbi, where are you staying?" Jesus responds "Come and see."

That response "Come and see" is more than just an offhand comment. It is his approach to the spiritual quest, not only in the Gospel of John but in the other gospels as well. In those gospels Jesus refuses to tell them who he is. Biblical scholars refer to this pattern in the Gospel of Mark as the Messianic secret. The disciples have to figure that out for themselves. Jesus encourages what we might call direct inquiry or a direct path of spiritual inquiry into his nature and our nature. He encouraged people to see for themselves.

John's gospel says that these two disciples – one of whom is identified as Andrew - follow Jesus to where he was staying. They spend the rest of the day and probably the night with him. It says they

25

"abided" with him. It even tells us what time it was when they entered the house – about 4 pm.

Things develop pretty quickly from there. Andrew goes to get his brother Simon and brings him to Jesus. Jesus takes a look at Simon and promptly gives him the nickname Cephas or Peter, which means Rock or Rocky. One wonders what it was about him that prompted this nickname. I picture him as the character played by Sylvester Stallone in the Rocky movies. He seems to be the same type of guy to me, not the smartest guy in the world but sincere.

The next day Jesus invites Philip to be his disciple with the simple words "Follow me." Philip goes off to find one of his friends named Nathanael, saying to him, "We have found Him of whom Moses in the Law and also the Prophets wrote — Jesus of Nazareth, the son of Joseph." Nathanael said to him, "Can any good thing come out of Nazareth?" Philip said to him, "Come and see." These are the same words Jesus uses. So Philip comes and sees.

"Jesus saw Nathanael coming to Him, and said of him, 'Behold, an Israelite indeed, in whom there is no deceit!' Nathanael said to Him, 'How do You know me?' Jesus answered and said to him, 'Before Philip called you, when you were under the fig tree, I saw you.' Nathanael answered Him, 'Rabbi, You are the Son of God; You are the King of Israel.' Jesus answered and said to him, 'Because I said to you that I saw you under the fig tree, do you believe? You will see greater things than these.' And He said to him, 'Truly, truly, I say to you, you will see the heavens opened and the angels of God ascending and descending on the Son of Man.'"

That last sentence is a reference to a story about Jacob in the Book of Genesis. Jacob had a dream of a stairway to heaven with angels going up and down. Jacob woke up and explained, "God is surely in this place and I did not know it. This is the house of God. This is the Gate of Heaven." In quoting that story, Jesus was saying that such an awakening experience lay ahead for Nathanael. The fact that Nathanael is under a tree is the symbolism of the axis mundi - also known as the Tree of Life, Bodhi tree and the Cross – all symbols of spiritual awakening.

Jesus was not into titles like Lamb of God, King of Israel, Son of God or even Messiah. He avoided titles and would not admit to them. Even when on trial for his life he avoided answering direct questions about who he claimed to be. But Christians get caught up in titles for Jesus. Christians go so far as to say that one has to believe certain titles for Jesus. You have to call him Son of God, God the Son, Christ, Lord, Savior, and even Lamb of God who takes away the sin of the world.

Jesus does not call himself any of those terms. The use of titles, names, labels and theology do not bring us any closer to knowing the identity of Jesus. In fact they can be distractions that stand in the way of seeing who Jesus is. Just because we use theologically correct titles, we think we know Jesus.

When it comes to the question of his identity, Jesus simply says, "Come and see." This is direct inquiry. Contemporary nonduality talks a lot about self-inquiry – knowing who we are. We certainly have that in the Gospel of John. John the Baptist goes into self-inquiry big time. But here it is about Christ inquiry or God inquiry. The gospel of nonduality is not about accepting what other people say about God or Jesus. That is secondhand faith. Nonduality is about coming and seeing for oneself.

It is significant that the original two disciples "come and see." It says that they abided with him. We find the same use of the term "abiding" in the wonderful story of two disciples who walked with Christ on the Emmaus Road on Easter day but did not recognize him. They came to their house and because it was becoming late, they invited the Stranger to abide with them as was the custom in the Middle East. He did, and in the abiding with him they recognized him. There is a wonderful Christian hymn about this.

Abide with me, fast falls the eventide
The darkness deepens Lord, with me abide
When other helpers fail and comforts flee
Help of the helpless, oh, abide with me

Swift to its close ebbs out life's little day
Earth's joys grow dim, its glories pass away
Change and decay in all around I see
O Thou who changest not, abide with me

Abiding with Christ or abiding in Christ is the Christian way of talking about abiding with the One who changest not. Abiding in the Eternal. Abiding in Awareness. Right beneath the surface of the Gospel of John there are repeated references to what we know as unitive awareness. There seems to be something about abiding in Christ's presence which communicates or imparts the grace of divine awareness. It is this experience of grace that prompted people to give Jesus titles.

But it is not about the titles. It is about the Kingdom of God, which is better translated the Divine Realm. It is about the Presence of God that was experienced in Jesus' presence. Jesus imparts this unitive awareness to those who follow him. I have an icon of Christ Pantocrator, which was made for me and given to me as a gift by an Eastern Orthodox iconographer I know. She made it for me as a way of thanking me for my spiritual leadership in my community. I was blessed to receive this gift, and it has a place of honor in my living room.

THE GOSPEL OF NONDUALITY

Like all icons the background is layered with gold leaf that shines whenever I look at it. The image is of Jesus, but what grabs my attention is the gold background behind Jesus. It communicates the divine spaciousness which is the True Nature of Christ. It is not about the image of Jesus as much as it is about the spacious divine presence from which the image emerges. The icon is a reminder that this divine spaciousness can be seen all the time in all things. There is the divine Reality from which all things come. This is our True Nature. This is what the person of Jesus Christ points to.

In the spiritual search people come looking for something or someone. When we see Reality, it is not something or someone. It simply is. I AM. The Ground of Being. Being Itself. We look to Jesus to lead us to this. Along the way we can get caught up in titles for Jesus and ideas about Jesus, which the Church assigns him. Don't get distracted by titles. It is about abiding in Christ. If you want to know Eternal Life, if you want to know Christ, if you want to know yourself, then come and see. When one inquires directly, then Divine Reality, which Jesus calls the Kingdom of God, is revealed.

TURNING WATER TO WINE

Jesus turned water into wine at a wedding in Cana, according to the much-loved story in the Gospel of John. It is the first of seven signs that Jesus does in this gospel. Jesus' family and disciples were invited to a wedding in Cana of Galilee, not far from Jesus' hometown of Nazareth. We are not told whose wedding it is, although it is safe to assume that it was a relative of Jesus. Jesus' mother seems to have a role in making sure the event goes off well. This means that it was likely a relative on Mary's side of the family - probably a cousin of Jesus.

The wedding is going fine when all of a sudden the wine runs out. This was obviously bad planning or a lack of funds, which does not reflect well on Mary or her family. Jesus' mother hurries over to Jesus and says, "They have no wine." Jesus responds in a manner that sounds rude, saying, "Woman, what does this have to do with me? My hour has not yet come."

Christian interpreters spend a lot of time trying to explain what appears to be Jesus rebuffing his mom. A good Jewish boy would not treat his mom rudely, we are told by preachers. Especially when this Jewish boy is Jesus. But why not? After all he was human! Jesus is expressing impatience. Mary, knowing her son's temperament, knows that Jesus will help. She says to the servants, "Do whatever he tells you."

We are told that there were six large water jars, which were used for ritual purification before eating, each jar able to hold twenty or thirty gallons of water. Jesus instructs the servants to fill the jars with water, draw off some of the contents, and bring it to the master of the feast. The Master of the Feast was an honorary position held by one of the invited guests, normally an important relative, who serves as master of ceremonies. He tastes the water (now turned to wine) and immediately calls the groom, saying to him. "Everyone serves the good wine first, and when people have drunk freely, then the poor wine. But you have kept the good wine until now."

This tale is usually interpreted as a miracle story that introduces the reader to Jesus' divine powers. It is actually a symbolic proclamation of Jesus as the Source of the Universe. The story points us to the opening words of the Gospel of John, which describes Jesus as the Word which "was with God and was God" and "through whom everything was made that was made."

This story of turning water to wine is a symbolic reenactment of the creation story with Jesus playing the role of the Creator. The creation story of Genesis starts with the earth covered with water, and the Spirit hovering over the face of the deep. God turns this watery chaos into life-sustaining cosmos with a word.

Here is Jesus as the Word doing the same sort of thing. With a word he turns the chaos of a wedding disaster into a memorable event that is still repeated 2000 years later. Without Jesus' intervention this wedding would have been a social catastrophe that would have disgraced this couple and their families.

Jesus turns tragedy into a blessing.

There are also echoes here of the Flood Story, which was a recreation of the world through watery chaos. The first thing that Noah does after the flood is plant a vineyard and make wine. This story of Jesus turning water into wine is meant to echo these Old Testament stories of creation and recreation. To Greek and Roman ears this wedding story would also have overtones of Dionysus, also called Bacchus. In Rome he was known as Liber Pater, (the Free Father), the Greco-Roman god of freedom and wine and celebration and joy.

Interpreting this story as nondualism, Jesus is pictured as the Divine Source from which all things originate. Christ is able to remake the world, symbolized by turning water into wine. We are free in the same way. The properties of this physical world are not as fixed as people think it is. To a great extent they are a matter of perception. Jesus' miracle may have been the transformation of people's perception more than the metamorphosis of water molecules.

Jesus was not a traveling magician, which were a shekel a dozen in those days. He was not a wizard saying a magic spell over jars of water like a first century Harry Potter. He doesn't lay his hands on the jars and pronounce a miracle like some TV evangelist. He tells the servants to fill the jars with water and bring some of the contents to the master of the feast, who then declares it to be the best wine he ever tasted. Everyone agrees.

Jesus was changing people's minds, opening them to a different way of perceiving reality. This was the wedding of a poor family that was cutting costs and hoping it would be sufficient to provide a decent wedding. They felt poor, and Jesus changed that into abundance! "Blessed are you who are poor, for yours is the kingdom of God." That is the miracle. That is what this story is communicating. Jesus changed the way the people saw reality that day. Life was wine instead of water.

This is the transformation that happens when we change from seeing this world as duality to seeing it as nondual. To read this story as nothing more than a miracle tale would make this "sign" into a parlor trick and Jesus into a sideshow performer. This is something much more fundamental. This is a sign proclaiming spiritual transformation. It is about seeing the world in a new way. Jesus was giving the wedding guests a glimpse into the nature of reality.

Our world is not the fixed mechanism that we perceive it to be. We peer out at the universe through five little pinholes called physical senses, which can discern only a miniscule portion of reality. We process this imperfect information through tiny simian brains and then declare we know the real world! How egotistical! Indian spirituality calls this perceived world maya or illusion. Our brains deceive us. This is demonstrated daily by the fact that millions of people believe in bizarre conspiracy theories like QAnon and Pizzagate and other fake news. Millions of people think Trump won the 2020 election! We know that people convince themselves of all sorts of things that are not true.

Humanity has convinced itself that we are alienated from the Divine and the world, lost and in need of liberation and salvation. We perceive our lives as suffering. We understand ourselves as miserable sinners under the judgment of a wrathful God who is going to send most of humanity into hell if they don't conform to certain religious demands.

That becomes our psychological and spiritual reality. Our reality is what we think it is, and we feel and act according. We feel we need to be liberated or saved. So we develop elaborate religious systems of beliefs and rituals to rescue ourselves from the prisons of our own making. These religious worlds become our emotional and psychological reality.

The truth is we are free. To realize that we are free is to wake up. As Jesus says later in this gospel, "When the Son sets you free, you are free indeed." We are liberated. We are saved. We are enlightened. There is nothing we have to do or believe to make it so. It is already reality.

The problem is that our minds think we are not free. So we search for freedom and salvation and enlightenment. We believe we are time bound creatures that are born and live and die. That is not what we are. We are not born and we do not die. We are the Eternal Source that can turn water into wine. Jesus knew this about himself and tried to communicate it to us. That is what this story is about.

Jesus knew himself to be the Eternal One. He proclaimed that we are also and can know that. This realization is eternal life. This is what the Gospel of John proclaims. That is what the seven I AM statements of Jesus communicate. This is what the seven signs of the Gospel of John point to. This first sign of turning water into wine is the first of these signs pointing to nondual truth.

JESUS WAS SPIRITUAL BUT NOT RELIGIOUS

Nonduality has more to do with spirituality than religion. Nonduality is certainly represented in the mystical branch of every religious tradition, but it tends to be relegated to the periphery of the religion. It is sometimes branded heresy and persecuted by the religion's powerbrokers, especially in Western religions. That was the case in Jesus' day. He was opposed by both the temple priests and the synagogue leaders of his own faith.

Jesus was a disrupter of what we would call today organized religion or the institutional church, especially the type that is in bed with worldly powers. Most western Christians do not see this antireligious theme in the ministry of Jesus because Christianity is still in bed with economic and political authorities. In America we need look no further than the Religious Right to see how conservative Christianity has sold its soul for political influence.

This is not unique to Christianity. It is true of every major religion that is large enough to gain social and political power in any country. It is true of Islam, Judaism, Hinduism and even Buddhism. In the second chapter of the Gospel of John we see

THE GOSPEL OF NONDUALITY

Jesus' attitude toward organized religion demonstrated in an action called the Cleansing of the Temple. Jesus takes a whip of cords and drives money-changers and sacrifice sellers out of the Jerusalem temple.

The Cleansing of the Temple is found in all four gospels, but it is somewhat different in the Gospel of John. First, in John's gospel it comes early in Jesus' ministry, whereas in the other three it comes in the last week of Jesus' life. In John it is his first public act after the wedding in Cana. It is his first symbolic action in Jerusalem and sets the theme of his ministry.

Second, what Jesus says as he drives them out is different. In the first three gospels Jesus says, "My Father's House shall be a house of prayer, but you have made it a den of thieves." He is attacking corruption in religion. In the Gospel of John he says this: "Take these things away; stop making My Father's house a house of business." This is variously translated a house of trade or a house of merchandise or a marketplace.

In the Greek text Jesus calls the temple an emporian, from which we directly get the word emporium. It is a place where business transactions take place. Jesus is his not just talking about corruption. He is talking about making religion into a business.

You can see why Christians today can't hear this message any longer. It is because many churches have become places of business. Big business in some cases – and I am thinking of megachurches, where pastors are more like CEOs. The pastors of such churches are the ones who like to be court prophets to presidents, although today we call them spiritual advisors. Jesus was crucified by such spiritual advisors. Remember the words of Jesus "You cannot serve both God and Mammon."

There is more controversy here in Jesus' words. He is not just condemning the role of business transactions in religion, he is addressing the idea of religion as a system of business transactions between God and humans. If you have been part of traditional Christianity, you know what I am talking about. In the dominant Christian theological systems the relationship between God and humans is pictured as a business transaction. We owe a debt to God which we cannot pay, so Jesus pays it for us.

Alternatively it is pictured as a legal transaction. We see this especially in the writings of Paul. We have broken the law and justice must be meted out. Punishment must be had, otherwise the cosmic order would fall apart, it seems. God can't just forgive. (Although we are never told why. If God is omnipotent, why can't God just forgive? But according to this religious system of thought, he can't.) His need for justice and punishment must be satisfied. So Jesus take the punishment for our sin upon himself, and we get off scot-free. We are never told how punishing an innocent person is just or fair, but that is how the story goes. Salvation is a transaction.

Christianity inherited this transactional model of salvation from Judaism. The sacrificial law of the Old Testament is a sin management system based on transactions that atone for sin and restore us to a proper relationship to God. Christianity continued the same pattern, only making Jesus into the sacrifice that pays our debt or atones for sin.

In the Cleansing the Temple, Jesus was doing away with this type of transactional religion. He was throwing out the whole sacrificial system, and by extension Christian sacrificial theology. He would not be the first Hebrew prophet to do this. God says in Jeremiah: "Your burnt offerings are not acceptable, nor your sacrifices pleasing to me."

Isaiah says: "What to me is the multitude of your sacrifices? says the LORD; I have had enough of burnt offerings of rams and the fat of well-fed beasts; I do not delight in the blood of bulls, or of lambs, or of goats. ... Bring no more vain offerings; incense is an abomination to me.... Your new moons and your appointed feasts my soul hates; they have become a burden to me; I am weary of bearing them."

God says in Amos: "I hate, I despise your feasts, and I take no delight in your solemn assemblies. Even though you offer me your burnt offerings and grain offerings, I will not accept them; and the peace offerings of your fattened animals, I will not look upon them. Take away from me the noise of your songs; to the melody of your harps I will not listen."

Jesus is repeating this anti-sacrificial theme of the Hebrew prophets, and he received the same response from the religious authorities as these prophets received. As Jesus said, "Jerusalem, Jerusalem! You kill the prophets and stone the messengers God has sent you!"

Jesus opposed dualistic religion conceived as a transaction between God and humans. He was opposed to the temple system, which he prophesied would come to an end with the destruction of the temple. This prophecy came to pass in 70 AD when Jerusalem was destroyed by the Romans. The temple has never been rebuilt, and the sacrificial system came to an end. In cleansing the temple, Jesus was symbolically ridding the earth and his own religion of such dualistic religion.

In place of temple religion Jesus understands humans as temples of God. God dwells in us. In this story the temple authorities challenge Jesus' authority to do this bold act. "So the Jews answered and said to Him, 'What sign do You show to us, since You do these things?' Jesus answered and said to them, 'Destroy this temple, and in three days I will raise it up.' Then the Jews said, 'It has taken forty-six years to build this temple, and will You raise it up in three days?' But He was speaking of the temple of His body."

In place of the business of religion complete with fancy buildings and priests and sacrifices, Jesus proposed a simple spirituality based on the indwelling Spirit of God in the human body. God is in us, not in buildings of stone. That idea is well attested in the New Testament. The apostle Paul wrote: "Don't you know that you yourselves are God's temple and that God's Spirit dwells in you?" This is incarnational nondual spirituality where there is no difference between the human body and God. To find God, we need only look within.

Jesus was spiritual but not religious. But didn't Jesus go to synagogue? Yes, he did, but the synagogue rulers were against him, and he was against them. When he preached in this hometown synagogue in Nazareth, they threw him out of the building and tried to throw him off a cliff. He only went into the synagogue to proclaim his radical alternative to the synagogue. I go to church regularly. I have spent my whole adult life pastoring churches, but that does not mean I buy into the dualistic distortions of organized religion. I attend church now because that is where I find community and where I can worship with fellow human beings.

Didn't Jesus go to the temple? Yes, he did. He went not to offer sacrifices but to teach in the temple courts his alternative gospel of a templeless spirituality, which reminds me a lot of Bonhoeffer's religionless Christianity. The message that Jesus proclaimed and lived was not about religion with its buildings, priesthood, sacrifices, laws and doctrines. He proclaimed a spirituality without duality, with no separation between God and humans that needed to be resolved through religious business or legal

THE GOSPEL OF NONDUALITY

transactions.

His gospel was about knowing what is in us. The closing verse of this chapter says, "Jesus had no need that anyone should testify of man, for He knew what was in man." Jesus knew what was in humans. He knew what was in him and in us. He knew and proclaimed that the Kingdom of God is within. God is in us. To know this is to know the gospel of Jesus Christ.

BORN AGAIN ... OR NOT

Evangelical Christians are not born again. With that sentence I began the second chapter of my book *Experiencing God Directly: The Way of Christian Nonduality*. That raised some eyebrows, as you can imagine! I will make the same declaration here. Evangelical Christians are not born again. They don't have any idea what Jesus meant by the phrase "born again." They are as clueless as Nicodemus.

What do evangelicals mean by the phrase "born again"? They mean that by the grace of God they have placed their faith in Jesus Christ as their personal Lord and Savior. They have trusted in Christ for salvation, often followed by being baptized in his name. That profession of faith may or may not be accompanied by a spiritual, religious or emotional experience.

Even though non-evangelicals think of being "born again" as a religious experience, it is more a profession of faith. Evangelicals would say that through trusting in Jesus, their sins have been forgiven and they have been saved by God's grace through faith in Christ. That - in a couple of sentences - is what most Evangelicals mean by being born again. That is not what Jesus meant by being born again. Here is the famous interchange between Jesus and the religious leader named Nicodemus as found in the third chapter of the Gospel of John.

"Now there was a man of the Pharisees named Nicodemus, a ruler of the Jews. This man came to Jesus by night and said to him, "Rabbi, we know that you are a teacher come from God, for no one can do these signs that you do unless God is with him." Jesus answered him, "Truly, truly, I say to you, unless one is born again he cannot see the kingdom of God." Nicodemus said to him, "How can a man be born when he is old? Can he enter a second time into his mother's womb and be born?" Jesus answered, "Truly, truly, I say to you, unless one is born of water and the Spirit, he cannot enter the kingdom of God. That which is born of the flesh is flesh, and that which is born of the Spirit is spirit. Do not marvel that I said to you, 'You must be born again.' The wind blows where it wishes, and you hear its sound, but you do not know where it comes from or where it goes. So it is with everyone who is born of the Spirit."
Nicodemus said to him, "How can these things be?" Jesus answered him, "Are you the teacher of Israel and yet you do not understand these things? Truly, truly, I say to you, we speak of what we know, and bear witness to what we have seen, but you do not receive our testimony. If I have told you earthly things and you do not believe, how can you believe if I tell you heavenly things?

What does Jesus mean here by the phrase "born again?" The phrase can be translated other ways, and some translations use the alternate phrases. It can be rendered "born anew" or "born from above." Jesus uses the phrase "born of the Spirit" in this passage. No matter how one translates it, Jesus tells Nicodemus that it means to "see the Kingdom of

God." Jesus answered him, "Truly, truly, I say to you, unless one is born again he cannot see the kingdom of God." Nicodemus immediately (probably intentionally) misunderstands Jesus to be talking about a physical rebirth. So Jesus explains that he is not talking about being born of the flesh again but born of the Spirit.

Nicodemus' preposterous idea of entering into the womb of his mother a second time is not as far off as it seems. We tend to reject and dismiss Nicodemus' idea as ridiculous. If taken literally it certainly is foolish, but when taken as a metaphor it has merit. That is why Jesus does not dismiss what Nick has to say. Jesus elsewhere said that one has to become like a little child to enter the Kingdom of God. A child in the womb is one with the mother. When we are born again we become like a little child again. The duality of separation is reversed and Unity is restored. That is what it means to be born again.

Those who are born again see the Kingdom of God. That is it. That is all Jesus says about what it means to be born again. Those who are not born again, don't see the Kingdom. There is no mention of a religious experience. No mention of having a personal relationship with Jesus as Lord and Savior. No mention of doctrines that have to be believed. All it means is being able to see the Kingdom of God.

Jesus says there is an element of mystery involved in this rebirth. "The wind blows where it wishes, and you hear its sound, but you do not know where it comes from or where it goes. So it is with everyone who is born of the Spirit." He seems to be saying that the origin and end of this second birth is unknown. It partakes of eternity and not of time – with no beginning and no end.

Jesus also talks about being born of water as well as the spirit. "Truly, truly, I say to you, unless one is born of water and the Spirit, he cannot enter the kingdom of God. That which is born of the flesh is flesh, and that which is born of the Spirit is spirit. Do not marvel that I said to you, 'You must be born again.'"

This has caused all sorts of theological and ecclesiastical arguments about whether or not Jesus is referring to baptism. It has given rise to the idea of "baptismal regeneration," meaning that baptism is the instrumental cause of the new birth. But it is uncertain that Jesus is talking about baptism here. He seems to be equating being born of water with being born of the flesh. So he may be referring to physical birth as being born of water, namely the breaking of the amniotic sac which marks the beginning of labor.

In any case it is clear that the distinguishing characteristic of this spiritual birth is the ability to see the Kingdom of God. He is speaking of spiritual sight, what Jesus often talks about as "having eyes to see." It is spiritual awareness of the all-pervading presence of the Divine that is called non-dual awareness. There is no duality. Heaven is seen on earth. As Elizabeth Barrett Browning puts it: "Earth's crammed with heaven, And every common bush afire with God, But only he who sees takes off his shoes."

Having one's eyes open to this spiritual reality is certainly like being born again. Just like an infant comes out of the dark womb into a whole new world, so does one who is born of the Spirt enter into a new world of Divine Light. It is a universe entirely different than normal waking consciousness. It is a spiritual world. The physical world still exists but only as an expression of the Divine. This new way of seeing is as different as day is from night. There is no vocabulary from the physical world that can accurately describe the spiritual.

This is the Kingdom of God that Jesus says is present in the world but people do not see it. It is the same Kingdom that Jesus says is within us and outside of us. These are sayings about the kingdom that are in the canonical gospels, but perhaps best exemplified in the non-canonical Gospel of Thomas. Life in this Kingdom of God is what the First Letter of John means by "being in the world but not of the world."

This unitive vision of the Kingdom of God did not become the customary understanding of the Kingdom of God in Christianity. In traditional Christianity the Kingdom came to be seen mainly as a physical kingdom coming to the earth in the future. Likewise the idea of the new birth came to be associated with religious conversion and baptism. But Jesus clearly says that the essential meaning of being born again is to undergo a transformation in which one is able to see the Kingdom of God and enter into the Kingdom of God.

How many evangelical Christians would say they see the Kingdom of God or have entered the Kingdom of God? I was a spiritual leader in Evangelicalism for decades, and I have never heard them speak in such terms. They speak about looking forward to the Kingdom of God in the future, either when Jesus physically returns to earth at the Second Coming or when they die and go to heaven. They do not talk about the Kingdom of God fully present here and now.

Faith in Jesus is wonderful. But it is not the new birth. It is not what it means to be born again. Being born again is having one's eyes opened to the Presence of the Kingdom of God all around us and within us. It is waking up to nondual Reality. It is like being raised from the dead. As a healed man says in the Gospel of John, "I was blind, but now I see!" It is a dramatic shift in perspective that is superbly described by the phrase born again, born anew, born from above, and born of the Spirit.

WHAT JOHN 3:16 REALLY MEANS

If there is one verse that Christians – especially evangelical Christians – know by heart it is John 3:16.

"For God so loved the world, that he gave his only begotten Son, that whosoever believeth in him should not perish, but have everlasting life." This verse is interpreted by Christians to mean that God loved us enough to offer Jesus on the cross as a sacrifice for sins. And if we receive Jesus as Lord and Savior then we are saved from judgment and hell and guaranteed a place in heaven after we die.

But when we look at it in the context of the verse, we see that is not what it means. There is no mention of the cross or sacrifice for sin. There is no mention of accepting Jesus into our hearts. There is no mention of Jesus as Lord and Savior. There is no mention of going to heaven after we die. All that is read into the passage by Christians. This verse is found in the context of spiritual awakening, which we looked at in the last chapter, and that is what it is talking about!

First of all it is about God's love for the world. "God so loved the world that he gave his only begotten Son." This verse extolls unconditional love, not God choosing a few elect souls while condemning the rest of humanity fry in hell. The very next verse says, "For God did not send the Son into the world to judge (or condemn) the world, but so that the world might be saved through Him." The verse is explicitly speaking against judgement.

The passage goes on to say that judgment is of our own making. It says, "And this is the judgment, that the Light has come into the world, and people loved the darkness rather than the Light." This is talking about ignorance and spiritual blindness. It is talking about people who are ignorant of the Kingdom of God which is right before their eyes now.

This is a message of unconditional love to all the world. "God so loved the world that he gave his only begotten Son." Giving his Son means sending Christ into the world. As the First Letter of John says, "In this was manifested the love of God toward us, because that God sent his only begotten Son into the world, that we might live through him." God giving his Son is not about God killing his Son through a barbaric act of torture. How can anyone call torturing and killing anyone, especially one's beloved Son, as love? The execution of Jesus was an act of religious violence and human hatefulness, not divine love.

The phrase "only begotten Son" is quoted by most Christians as proof that Christians alone have the true religion. They say that Jesus is the only begotten Son of God, whereas the founders of other religions are merely human religious teachers ... at best, if not imposters, false teachers and instruments of Satan! This makes Christianity number one in their eyes – the only true faith! Christians use other verses to bolster the claim to exclusivity, such as Jesus' famous words: "I am the Way, the Truth, and the Life. No one comes to the Father but through me." That verse is interpreted to mean that Jesus is the only way, and only Christians have Jesus.

Nothing could be further from the Truth. When Christ says in the Gospel of John that no one comes to the Father but through him, he is speaking as the Eternal Christ, the Logos introduced in the Prologue of John. All Christ's words in the Gospel of John are Christ speaking as the Logos, the Preexistent Eternal Cosmic Universal Christ. Christ says that the only way to Life is through his Eternal Nature as the Logos, the Word, which enlightens every person who comes into the world.

The phrase "only begotten" is best translated as "one and only," and that is how most English translations render it. "One and only" refers to the Original Oneness, the One without a second, from which the universe came. Others call this nonduality. The Prologue says that everything was made through this One.

Many Christians assume this phrase "only begotten Son" is a reference to the physical birth of Jesus and especially the virgin birth. They say that Jesus was sired by God the Father, and that is the only time this ever happened, which makes Jesus God's only begotten son. That is not what "only begotten son" means. Any Christian pastor familiar with church history, the early church councils and creeds knows this. This phrase does not refer to the birth of Jesus but his eternal origin. Christian theologians say that Christ was "begotten before all ages." The Nicene Creed says: "We believe in one Lord Jesus Christ, the only begotten Son of God, begotten of the Father before all worlds, [or "before all ages,"] Light of Light, very God of very God, begotten, not made."

This begottenness of the Eternal Christ is from eternity. It is not talking about the physical birth of Jesus of Nazareth. The Universal Christ is the One from which all else comes, including all other sons and daughters of God. This One and Only Son gives us power to become children of God, born of God, as the Prologue says.

"For God so loved the world, that he gave his only begotten Son, that whosoever believeth in him should not perish, but have everlasting life." Everlasting life – better translated Eternal Life - is Unitive awareness. Believing in Christ is trusting this awareness. It is what theologian Paul Tillich calls "absolute faith," which is very different from personal faith.

When Christians – especially the conservative and evangelical variety - talk about believing in Christ, they mean receiving Jesus into their hearts, thereby beginning a personal relationship with Jesus Christ. This involves at least an elementary understanding of who Jesus is and what he did. Notice that none of that is mentioned in this chapter. These ideas are imported into the text by Christians, who then read it out of the text, without being aware of their circular reasoning.

The word "believe" is not about believing things about Jesus. To "believe in" means to have faith in, to trust in, or entrust oneself to. It means to give oneself to completely, so there is no self left. The Greek text actually says "believing into him." Believing into the Eternal Christ means going into Christ, giving oneself wholly to the One and Only. It means surrendering to Primordial Oneness that is the Eternal Logos we know as I AM.

This is not a onetime conversion experience sometime in the past, the way Christians interpret it. Not to get too Greeky here (which is always a temptation for us preachers who studied Greek in seminary) but the Greek word for believe used here is a present active participle, indicating an action ongoing in the present. It is best translated "believing." It is happening now. "Whoever believing in him shall not perish but have eternal life."

I exercise this absolute faith every day in meditation and throughout the day. In meditation I let my thoughts settle enough to see clearly. Then I notice Presence, unitive awareness, the Ground of Being that is always present as the background music of life. When this is recognized, I relax into it. I lean into this. Leaning back into Him. I entrust my small human self, my psychological self, unto this Presence that is Christ. When I ease back into Christ, I cease to be my self, and I see the world as the True Self, who is Christ.

I liken this to being on a boat in one of the clear freshwater lakes here in New Hampshire. When I am on the boat I am aware of the water beneath me and all around me upholding me, although it is easy to get distracted and forget about it. Whenever I want I can stop and jump into the fresh clean cool water. That is what meditation is like. I take the time to sit on a cushion and be consciously aware of Nondual Reality that is always in the background of life. I sit down to meditate and spiritually dive into it. I entrust myself to the water. That dive is faith. That is "believing into" the Eternal Christ. That is believing in the Name of I AM. That is Nondual Awareness.

This action is something that the little human self does. It is ceasing to act as a self, so that Large Self can consciously present. Taoism calls this wu wei, non-action or wei wu wei, action without action. This non-action of relaxing back into Christ is faith. Life is seen as Eternal Life, Divine Life, Everlasting Life. When one eases into one's True Nature, the distinction between oneself and Christ disappears. One is seen as just a drop of water in the lake. There is only Christ, who is all and in all.

To know this is Eternal Life. As the final words of this chapter says, "The one who believes into the Son has eternal life." God so loves the world, that he gives his one and only Son, that whoever is believing in him does not perish – does not die when the human self or human body dies - but has everlasting life now. This is what John 3:16 means.

DRINKING FROM THE WELL OF NONDUALITY

In the fourth chapter of the Gospel of John, Jesus meets a Samaritan woman at a well. It is a powerfully symbolic story. Jesus and his disciples were traveling from Jerusalem, where they had observed the Passover, back to Galilee in the northern part of the country. To do so he traveled through a middle region called Samaria. That route is significant in itself. This region was occupied by Samaritans, who were of a different religion and race than Jews. They considered each other heretics. Most Jews went out of way to avoid traveling through Samaria, but Jesus felt no qualms about the direct route.

He arrived at a town called Sychar at noontime. While his disciples were off getting some lunch, Jesus sat by the town well. A Samaritan woman came to draw water from the well, and he engaged her in conversation. At first it was simply a request for a drink of water from the well, but the conversation soon turned to spiritual matters.

This story is filled with dualities. It is a living illustration of the Yin Yang symbol. Here is a man and a woman, a Jew and a Samaritan, two different races and two different religions. They come together at an ancient and deep well which had been dug by Jacob, the forefather of Israel. The well symbolizes what Jesus calls "living water."

These two people were drawing nourishment from the same Source, symbolizing the single Source from which all religions draw their inspiration. It is marvelous symbolism. Their conversation is about how Truth is deeper than religious, cultural and racial barriers.

Jesus asks the woman for a drink of water. "Then the woman of Samaria said to Him, 'How is it that You, being a Jew, ask a drink from me, a Samaritan woman?' For Jews have no dealings with Samaritans. Jesus answered and said to her, 'If you knew the gift of God, and who it is who says to you, "Give Me a drink," you would have asked Him, and He would have given you living water.'"

Here is a Jew asking a Samaritan for water. Here is the Christ – the founder of the Christian faith - asking a woman of another faith and race and culture. For Christians reading this it means that we need not be hesitant to look for spiritual nourishment outside of our own religious tradition.

I have been nourished throughout my life by other religious traditions. In my late teens and early twenties I was reading the Tao Te Ching, the Upanishads and the Bhagavad-Gita. I was learning from Chinese Philosophy, Buddhism, Hinduism and Islam. I cannot imagine what my life would have been like without these influences.

To read only within one's own religious tradition is like eating only one type of food. Maybe that is alright for some people, but I love all types of food - Chinese food, Italian food, French food and Mexican food. Okay, maybe not Mexican food, but you get my point.

In the story both the Jew and the Samaritan were

drinking from the same well. All spiritual traditions draw from the same eternal Source, which has been called the Perennial Philosophy by Aldous Huxley. Religions draw water using different types of vessels, but it is the same living water. They express truth differently, but in the differences we can see the commonality. Jesus calls this commonality Living Water.

The Samaritan woman did not see this commonality at first. She was so attached to the outward forms of her religion that she missed the inner Truth. We see this attitude in her words. First she accused Jesus of claiming to be greater than her ancestor Jacob, from which the Samaritans traced their lineage. She goes on to point out the differences between their types of worship, saying, "Our fathers worshiped on this mountain, and you Jews say that in Jerusalem is the place where one ought to worship."

Jesus responds, "Woman, believe Me, the hour is coming when you will neither on this mountain, nor in Jerusalem, worship the Father. ... The hour is coming, and now is, when the true worshipers will worship the Father in spirit and truth.... God is Spirit, and those who worship Him must worship in spirit and truth."

Jesus is referring to spirituality that transcends religion. Jesus was a Jew and he unapologetically prefers his own spiritual tradition. He says to her, "You worship what you do not know; we know what we worship, for salvation is of the Jews." Jesus was man of this time and culture. He never abandoned his religion and had no intention of starting a new religion. I am a Christian, and I have no desire to abandon my religion. Hindus think their tradition is the best because it is most inclusive. Buddhists think theirs is the clearest. These days Nondualists think their approach is the purest and best. We all are products of our religious backgrounds and spiritual experiences. That is good, as long as we see that all traditions are united in a deeper Reality.

We live in a world of duality, and that means differences, including different religions. Jesus says that "the hour is coming, and now is, when the true worshipers will worship the Father in spirit and truth... God is Spirit, and those who worship Him must worship in spirit and truth." The woman glimpses the truth in Jesus' words and declares Jesus to be a prophet. I agree. Jesus was able to see a time in the future when the duality of dueling religions would be transcended. I think we are beginning that time now.

Jesus says that those who drink from the waters of religious duality will thirst again. They will have to come back again and again through religious rituals and spiritual practices to be refreshed. Jesus offers another way. He says, "Whoever drinks of this water will thirst again, but whoever drinks of the water that I shall give him will never thirst. But the water that I shall give him will become in him a fountain of water springing up into everlasting life." The woman said to Him, "Sir, give me this water, that I may not thirst, nor come here to draw."

Jesus is contrasting inner spirituality with external religion. In the story the woman left her waterpot at the well when she returned to the town. This is symbolic. She had drank from the living water and did not need the drinking vessel any longer, which symbolize the externals of religion. As the Buddha said, once one has reached the other shore, one no longer needs the boat.

True spirituality comes from within. Jesus says elsewhere, "The Kingdom of God is within you." It is not found in religious beliefs and practices. Those can be expressions of the inner reality, imperfectly communicating the inexpressible. But duality can never adequately express nonduality. It needs to be known directly. That is what Jesus is pointing to in his conversation with the woman at the well. Jesus is instructing the woman to look within. Jesus asked the woman about her identity. That self-inquiry was the path to realizing Truth. It becomes clear that Jesus knows this woman better than she knows herself.

This woman was willing to go beyond self-deceit and the layers of psychological injuries and social ostracism that she had endured. It is clear from the details of the story that this woman was an outcast in her own community. That is why she was visiting the well in the heat of the day, when all respectable women were sheltering in the shade. She was an outsider. She was scarred and hurting. She was psychologically and spiritually thirsty. That is why she asked Jesus for living water. This is the type of person who is open to Living Water. As Jesus said, "Blessed are those who hunger and thirst for righteousness, [spiritual wholeness] for they shall be satisfied."

The end of the story loops back to the identity of Jesus. At the beginning of their conversation Jesus had said to the woman, "If you knew the gift of God, and who it is who says to you, 'Give Me a drink,' you would have asked Him, and He would have given you living water." At the end of the encounter the woman suspects that Jesus is the Messiah and says so. Jesus' response is, "I who speak to you am He." At least that is how it is normally translated.

Here is a place where it is helpful to consult the Greek text. The first two words of Jesus' response is "I AM." This is one of the many "I AM" statements that run throughout the Gospel of John. Jesus literally says, "I AM is speaking to you." The New Living Translation brings out this literal meaning, translating it: "The 'I AM' is here." Jesus identifies himself as the Eternal One, who is the Living Water. As Jesus says a few chapters later: "If anyone thirsts, let him come to me and drink. He who believes in me, as the Scripture has said, out of his heart will flow rivers of living water."

There is more to this story. I have barely dipped my toes into the water, you might say. But I hope the reader sees the main points. Jesus was a spiritual teacher who was able to take a chance encounter at a town well and turn it into a session of spiritual direction that pointed a woman to her True Nature and his True Nature. This is the Nondual Reality that transcends religious, gender and cultural identities. This is the water of life at the heart of all spiritual traditions.

ALREADY WHOLE

In chapter five of John's Gospel, we find a story of Jesus healing a man at the Pool of Bethesda in Jerusalem. It is much more than just a miracle tale. Like all the stories about Jesus in the Gospel of John, this is intended as symbolic. It is proclaiming the ultimate healing that comes by realizing one's true Self and waking up to the Truth of Eternal Life.

Jesus was in Jerusalem again for one of the Jewish feasts. He comes into Jerusalem through the Sheep Gate to the Pool of Bethesda, where people were gathered to be healed. It was thought that the waters of this pool had miraculous powers at certain times during the holy days. People believed that an angel of the Lord came down and stirred the waters of the pool, and whoever got into the water first after that would be healed.

There was a man lying there who had been sick 38 years. We are not told what his condition was, which indicates that he represents all people. Jesus saw the man lying there and said to him, "Do you want to be made whole?" The sick man answered Him, "Sir, I have no man to put me into the pool when the water is stirred up. While I am coming, another steps down before me." At that point Jesus simply says to him,

"Rise, take up your bed and walk." Immediately the man was whole, picked up his bed, and walked.

On the surface this is a healing miracle, but it is really a parable about being made whole in a spiritual sense. I use the phrase "being made whole" in a literal sense. We are not isolated parts of the whole, tiny psychological entities encased in human bodies of flesh. We are the whole. To wake up to the wholeness is to enter Kingdom of God.

Jesus asks the man in this story, "Do you want to be made whole?" The intention of the man is important. The Buddha called it "right intent." Most people do not really want to be made whole. They have gotten used to the way things are. Most people have no true desire for liberation, freedom, salvation or enlightenment. We prefer bondage, and we spend our lives escaping from freedom, as Erich Fromm phrased it.

People convince themselves that there is something intrinsically wrong with them, a fundamental dis-ease in their souls. Different spiritual traditions use different words and concepts to explain what is thought to be wrong. Hindus call it ignorance or bondage. Buddhists call it dukkha or suffering. Christians call it sin and original sin. We are born in this condition, Christianity says. Calvinists call it total depravity. Christians see the world as fallen and we along with it. Humankind is said to have fallen from a primordial paradise into a condition of lostness, sin, death and condemnation. It is a dark view of the human condition.

The man in the story has convinced himself that his case is hopeless. He has been sick all his life and has come to accept that his situation will never change. When Jesus asked him, "Do you want to be made whole?" he does not reply the way that we would expect. He does not say, "Yes, please, I do, with all my heart and soul!" Instead he gives Jesus an excuse why it is impossible that he will ever be whole.

Jesus does not accept his diagnosis or prognosis. Jesus sees the man's innate wholeness and calls him to act upon it. Jesus tells him, "Rise, take up your bed, and walk." The man does exactly that. The story does not say that Jesus healed him. Jesus simply tells him to get up, and he did!. All it took was someone to tell him that he was able to get up.

I am not saying that all physical ailments are in our heads or that illness is just a misunderstanding. Such a spiritual philosophy has caused some religious people to not seek medical treatment for themselves or their children. Too many lives have been needlessly lost due to that understanding of illness. That is not what this story is teaching, and it is certainly not what I am teaching.

In one sense illness is unreal, but only in the sense that the whole physical universe is unreal in an ultimate sense. The only ultimate reality is God. Everything else is transitory. Everything else comes and goes. Only that which does not change is real in an ultimate sense. Our physical existence comes and goes, and therefore it is not real in this ultimate sense. The same with the conditions of this temporary body. But while we are living as temporary mortals in this physical world we need to seek help in this world. That means that when we become ill, we seek medical attention.

But this story is not just about physical healing. It is a parable about how to be saved from spiritual disease and suffering. Jesus showed this man that he already was whole. Jesus pointed that out to the man by telling him to get up and carry his cot away from that place, a place that reinforced his belief in his own brokenness and helplessness.

The truth is we are already whole. The goal of all religious traditions is already a reality. We are already saved, already free from bondage, already awake. We are one with Ultimate Reality beyond this physical world. All spiritual systems propose some goal of wholeness (holiness). This man had the goal of getting into the water at just the right time to be healed. Jesus showed this man that he did not need to get in the water; he was whole just the way he was. All he had to do was get to his feet, and carry away his cot - the symbol of his bondage. That is exactly what the man did. He arose, picked up his cot and walked away.

The Gospel says that as a result of this healing and Jesus' subsequent teaching about it, "Therefore the Jews sought all the more to kill Him, because He not only broke the Sabbath [because he did this healing on the Sabbath], but also said that God was His Father, making Himself equal with God."

They clearly heard Jesus teaching that he was equal with God, saying that his own true nature was divine. Jesus makes it clear that this is all of humanity's true nature as well, insofar as they realize they are one with Him. Being one in Christ means being one with God. That is wholeness. It is to see who Jesus really is and who we really are.

Jesus said to the religious leaders who were accusing him of heresy, "You search the Scriptures, for in them you think you have eternal life; and these are they which testify of Me. But you are not willing to come to Me that you may have life." This gives us insight into Jesus' approach to scripture.

All major religions have scriptures, whether it be the Muslims' Quran, the Jews' Tanakh, the Buddhists' Sutras, the Hindu's Vedas, or the Christians' Bible. They see their scriptures as inspired. People find guidance from the Divine in their Scriptures. But in time Scriptures become substitutes for the Divine. Instead of people going directly to the One to whom the scriptures point, people think that the Scriptures themselves contain eternal life.

That is secondhand spirituality. I have seen this in my own tradition when evangelical Christians apply terms like "infallible" and "inerrant" to the Bible. They insist that people must take everything these ancient writers said literally, even when it comes to science and history. This means literally believing in things like seven day creation, talking serpents and donkeys, the sun standing still, and floating axe heads.

Jesus refutes that view of Scripture. He says, "You search the Scriptures, for in them you think you have eternal life; and these are they which testify of Me. But you are not willing to come to Me that you may have life." The purpose of Scripture is to point people beyond itself to the Eternal One, so that they may share in Eternal Life.

But many Christians miss the point and do not come to the Eternal Christ. Instead they settle for theological systems about Christ. They fabricate elaborate schemes of salvation that involve accepting certain doctrines and practices. Other religions do the same thing with their beliefs and practices. But all those are unnecessary. Like the man at the pool of Bethesda, we already have what we seek. We are what we seek. We are already whole. All we have to do is get up and walk. It is just a matter of accepting it and trusting it. This story points us to that One Reality.

COMMUNION AND NONDUALITY

The Lord's Supper is a symbol of unitive awareness, which Jesus called the Kingdom of God. This ritual, also called Holy Communion or the Eucharist, is a symbolic proclamation of nonduality. Of course, that is not the way it is presented in traditional Christianity. But that is the way the Gospel of John presents it.

This sacrament is said to commemorate the Last Supper that Jesus had with his disciples, which was a Passover Meal. At least that is how the meal is portrayed in the first three gospels of the New Testament. But in the Gospel of John the Last Supper is not a Passover Meal. Furthermore the Lord's Supper is not instituted at the Last Supper in the Fourth Gospel. There is no mention of bread or wine. Nothing is said about his body or blood.

John's Gospel changes the calendar of events surrounding Jesus' death so that the Passover Meal does not happen until after Jesus dies. John does this deliberately so that the Lord's Supper would not be interpreted as a sacrificial meal with all the theological ramifications that implies. At the Last Supper, instead of a ritual of bread and wine interpreted as the body and blood of Christ, a different ritual is established. It is the ritual of foot-washing, which communicates the importance of serving one another in humility.

At the time that John was written, the "body and blood" interpretation of the Lord's Supper had already been widely adopted by the early church. So the Fourth Gospel tries to reinterpret it. This reveals that there was an alternate understanding of the Eucharist in the early church. There was a minority voice that saw the Eucharist not as sacrifice for sins but as union with God. That is why one of the terms used to describe it is Communion, which literally means "union with."

In John's Gospel Jesus' discussion of his body and blood is placed earlier in Jesus' ministry in the context of the feeding of the Five Thousand in chapter 6. The Feeding of the 5000 plays the role of the Lord's Supper in John's Gospel. Jesus is not offering the food in this story. Instead it is provided by a young boy, thereby echoing Jesus' teaching that we have to become like a young child to enter the Kingdom of God. The meal for the Five Thousand was not a Jewish family ritual like the Passover meal. It was an outdoor picnic with friends and strangers. It celebrates the abundance that happens when people offer what they have to others. This meal came to be called the Love Feast in Christianity, mentioned in the little Book of Jude.

It is an entirely different way of approaching the Lord's Table. For John it is a symbol of everyday living that reveals the abundant presence of God. It teaches us what it means to abide in Christ in union with God in what I call unitive awareness. Using the theological vocabulary of the Gospel of John, this is about the eternal I AM in Christ and us.

In the context of the Feeding of the 5000, Jesus' offers one of his I AM statements, which is shorthand for spiritual identity with the Divine. This is the pattern in the Fourth Gospel: sign and sermon. Jesus does a miracle – called a sign – and then gives a sermon that explains the meaning of the sign. Each of those sermons includes an I AM statement in which Jesus proclaims his true nature as Eternal Being. His words echo the story of God revealing his eternal nature and name to Moses at the Burning bush.

Jesus feeds thousands of people with a few little rolls of bread and fish, and then declares, "I am the Bread of Life." He calls himself the Living Bread and the Bread that has come down from Heaven. In his sermon he draws a parallel to the manna that the Hebrews ate in the wilderness after their escape from Egypt. Jesus says, "I am the bread of life. Your fathers ate the manna in the wilderness, and are dead. This is the bread which comes down from heaven, that one may eat of it and not die. I am the living bread which came down from heaven. If anyone eats of this bread, he will live forever." Just like the manna in the wilderness gave the Hebrews' physical life, so does the bread of life give spiritual life. Then just so there would be no doubt that this passage is talking about the Lord's Supper, Jesus explicitly speaks about his body and blood.

Jesus said to them, "Most assuredly, I say to you, unless you eat the flesh of the Son of Man and drink His blood, you have no life in you. Whoever eats My flesh and drinks My blood has eternal life, and I will raise him up at the last day. For My flesh is true food, and My blood is true drink. He who eats My flesh and drinks My blood abides in Me, and I in him. As the living Father sent Me, and I live because of the Father, so he who feeds on Me will live because of Me. This is the bread which came down from heaven—not as your fathers ate the manna, and are dead. He who eats this bread will live forever."

Such language about eating his flesh and blood can be offensive to people. That has prompted nonsacramental groups like the Quakers and Unitarians to abandon the rite. I have had parishioners in my churches refuse to partake of Communion for this reason. They have described it to me as a pagan ritual. Historians tell us that the ritual has parallels in pagan mystery cults during the time Christianity was forming. Ritual consumption of a god was widely practiced by religious groups. Osiris, Dionysus, Attis and others were ritually consumed by their devotees. Although the early development of the Lord's Supper was likely influenced by the religious practices of its Greco-Roman culture, it was drawing primarily upon the sacrificial motifs of the Hebrew Bible, where a sacrificial meal was eaten.

But whatever its origin, ritually eating Jesus' flesh and drinking his blood is not a pleasant imagery, especially when practiced on a regular basis in a worship service. Most Christians are so used to the ritual that we don't think about how it must appear to outsiders. The early Christians had to deal with charges of cannibalism, which is why John's gospel omits the Lord's Supper in its story of the Last Supper and substitutes the more acceptable ritual of foot washing.

In the Gospel of John the elements of the Eucharist are called "true food" and "true drink" or Food of Truth and Drink of Truth. John's Gospel interprets the Lord's Supper as about Truth and abiding in Christ. Jesus says, "My flesh is true food, and My blood is true drink. He who eats My flesh and drinks My blood abides in Me, and I in him. As the living Father sent Me, and I live because of the Father, so he who feeds on Me will live because of Me."

Communion is about being one with Christ. That

is the meaning of Jesus' phrase "abide in me." This is also translated "dwell in me" or "live in me." This same truth is proclaimed in the synoptic gospels when Jesus says that the kingdom of God is within us. In the Gospel of John Jesus explores what it means to "abide in him" in greater detail in what is called his High Priestly Prayer in chapter 17, which he offers on the night of the Last Supper. I will deal with that more in a later chapter.

Abiding in Christ is nondual awareness. When my mind rests from the fleeting images and ideas of the world, I abide alone in the Eternal Christ that does not change. That is also the awareness communicated in the Lord's Supper. I abide in Christ. I identify with the Eternal Christ. The two become one because they are one. Just like physical food become incorporated into our physical body, so we are one with Christ in the Lord's Supper.

That is why I prefer the term Communion for the Lord's Supper. Abiding in Christ is not just a ritual or a spiritual practice. It is everyday awareness. It is always present. It is the undercurrent of our consciousness, which only needs our attention to come to the forefront. This is nondual awareness. This is what we are. We are one with God, abiding in Christ, no matter what we are doing. That is why Brother Lawrence could say he was as close to God in the monastery kitchen washing dishes as on his knees at the Eucharist. We are one with Christ in God. That is the meaning of the Lord's Supper.

I AM

In this chapter I am going to deal with the most important statement spoken by Jesus in the Gospel of John. It is found in John 8:58. Everything so far has led up to this verse, and everything after it is based upon it. It is the pinnacle of the gospel. They are words Jesus spoken in response to repeated inquiries by people concerning who he was. They asked whether he was the Messiah or the Prophet or someone else. Jesus responded, "Most assuredly, I say to you, before Abraham was, I AM."

To interpret this saying properly it needs to be placed in context. Chapters 7 and 8 center on a discussion of the identity of Jesus, explored in the context of the Feast of Tabernacles. Jesus is once again in Jerusalem for one of the Jewish feasts. This time it is the Feast of Tabernacles, which commemorates the time that the Hebrews spent in the wilderness after they left Egypt in the Exodus and before they came into the promised land.

During this feast Jesus spent time in the temple teaching. Jesus had already called himself the Bread of Life, which he compared to the manna that God gave to the Hebrews during this wilderness time. Then at the culmination of the feast, Jesus said, "If anyone thirsts, let him come to Me and drink. He who believes in Me, as the Scripture has said, out of his heart will flow rivers of living water." This is a reference to the miracle of God bringing water out of a rock in the wilderness. It also echoes the scene earlier when Jesus spoke to the Samaritan woman about living water.

Then Jesus gives another one of his I AM statements, saying, "I am the light of the world. He who follows Me shall not walk in darkness, but have the light of life." Jesus was referring to the pillar of fire that lighted the way for the Hebrews during their time in the wilderness. All these references to the Feast of Tabernacles go back to the opening chapter of this Gospel, when the prologue said that God tabernacled among us in the person of Jesus. "And the Word became flesh and dwelt (literally "tabernacled") among us (literally "in us").

Jesus was in the temple teaching and said, "And you shall know the truth, and the truth shall make you free." That was another reference to the liberation of the Exodus. Then the conversation turned from Moses and the wilderness to Abraham. Jesus gets into a heated argument with the religious authorities, at one point calling them children of the devil. You can imagine that they did not take that accusation well. They retort that Jesus is a Samaritan and has a demon. They question Jesus' right to say the things he does. They ask, "Are You greater than our father Abraham, who is dead? And the prophets are dead. Who do you make yourself out to be?"

Jesus responds, "Your father Abraham rejoiced to see my day, and he saw it and was glad." Then the Jews said to Him, "You are not yet fifty years old, and have you seen Abraham?" Jesus said to them, "Most assuredly, I say to you, before Abraham was, I AM." Abraham lived 2000 years before Jesus, yet he said, "Before Abraham was, I AM."

Traditionally this statement is interpreted as a reference to Jesus' preexistence as the Eternal Logos, introduced to us in the first verse of the gospel. Jesus is equating himself with the Divine Name spoken to Moses at Sinai. That would have been enough to get him executed for heresy, although that will not get you accused of heresy in Christianity any longer. It is considered orthodoxy. But what Jesus is really teaching will get you accused of heresy today.

Jesus was not just talking about himself. He was talking about all humans. A few verses earlier he called himself the Son of Man, which is an express that means "a human." He was speaking as a representative of humankind. In his bold I AM statement Jesus was teaching about human nature. He was teaching about our nature. For us to call ourselves I AM will get us attacked by church authorities in every generation. What Jesus said of himself is true of every human being because we are one with Christ. We not separate individuals. Each one of us can say with Jesus, "Before Abraham was, I AM."

This saying of Jesus is equivalent to a Zen koan. A famous koan says, "Show me your original face before you were born." Or "Show me your original face before your mother and father were born." Jesus' koan "Before Abraham was, I AM" is pointing to the same reality. Koans are meant to direct our attention to our essential nature apart from our physical human manifestations.

What were you before you were you? What were you before you were born? Better yet, before you were conceived? Before your parents were born? What were you before the universe was born? You were obviously not your physical body. You were not the psychological self. That was formed by your brain in interaction with the environment during the early years of life. What were you before the earth was formed? Don't be tempted to engage in metaphysical speculation about the individual soul before birth – transmigration and reincarnation and all that stuff. Those are just ideas. Keep this to direct awareness of what you are now and always have been. What were you before you were born?

If you have no idea what I am talking about, congratulations! You are on the right track. This is not an intellectual exercise! If you are still flummoxed, wonderful! This is about unknowing. If when you look at your original face you see nothing, even better! It is literally no thing. If you sense your original nature as everything, great! Sense what you were before you were you. Fall back into it. Rest in it. This is what you are now.

This is our self-identity that cannot be denied. Everything else can be denied but not I AM. I am that I am. I am and always have been and always will be. God identified himself to Moses as, "I am that I am." It can be variously translated "I will be what I will be" or "I am the Eternal One." The Exodus story pictures God speaking these words to Moses through a burning bush, but that is symbolic. This I AM was burning within Moses. This is Moses' self-revelation of spiritual reality. At that moment, Moses woke up to his true identity.

This Self-identity is available to all. This is our experiential reality. See who you truly are. What is Real is what does not change, like the burning bush that does not burn out. It has nothing to do with this temporal world. It is what you were before this temporal world, what you be will after your mortal body dies. That is what you are! Many people are anxious about death, wondering what – if anything - comes after death. This is what comes after death because it was before death and it is now. Death is conquered through I AM. Rest in that eternal, timeless identity here now.

This may seem difficult to realize in experience, but it is actually the easiest thing possible because it is what you really are. How much easier can it be than to be what you are? There is nothing to do. Nothing to see. Nothing to think about. Just step back from the masks we wear and the ideas that fill the mind. Step back and rest into our eternal existence. Rest in Being. The Ground of Being. Being Itself. Spirit. Eternity. This is not existence, which is fleeting and temporary, but Being from which existence comes. Do not be a person with a name or a role. Just be. It is not about "I am this" or "I am that." It is just I AM.

This is not a mystical state of consciousness to be achieved by spiritual disciplines. This is simple awareness. It is the sense of Self that is at the root of existence. You know this truth intuitively. Everyone knows this reality naturally. People just overlook it because it is so primary, so much more basic than our fabricated identities based on body and mind. This is not body or mind. This is before body or mind and after body and mind, but includes body and mind. Some call it Self, God or Christ. It is what Jesus was referring to when he said, "Before Abraham was, I am." This is nonduality. "That thou art," as the Upanishads say.

Jesus proclaimed these words of Self-Realization to the religious leaders of his day, and it got him killed. Jesus repeatedly said in chapters 7 and 8 that people were going to kill him. It is because of this simple statement "I AM" that they wanted him dead, thinking that would kill the message. But today they are dead and the message remains. Religion cannot kill Truth. This radical I AM statement is the heart of all true spirituality. It is a window into the Divine and our true nature. It is present here now. See for yourself the truth of the words: Before Abraham was,

I am.

SPIRITUAL SIGHT

Before they were called prophets, Christ (anointed one), buddha (awakened one), jnani (knowing one), or arhat (worthy one), they were called seers. The Hebrew Scriptures say this was the term used in the time of the prophet Samuel. It reads, "The prophet of today was formerly called the seer." Such people were able to see with spiritual eyes what could not be seen with physical eyes. Jesus called this being "born again." He said, "Unless one is born again he cannot see the Kingdom of God." It can be called spiritual sight.

In the ninth chapter of the Gospel of John there is a story of Jesus healing a man born blind. On the surface it is about physical blindness and physical healing, but Jesus makes it clear that it is really about spiritual sight and spiritual healing. It is not about being visually impaired but being spiritually impaired.

This story addresses the psychological barriers to seeing the Kingdom of God. Seeing the Kingdom of God is another term for spiritual awakening, enlightenment, liberation or salvation. Seekers can become frustrated when they don't seem to be able to see this nondual Reality. Many may have been on a spiritual quest for years – perhaps all their lives – and they still don't see it. For that reason Jesus addresses this issue first.

Jesus encounters a man who had been physically blind from birth. His disciples asked Him, "Rabbi, who sinned, this man or his parents, that he was born blind?" Do you hear the guilt in the question? The disciples are trying to find someone to blame for the condition of this man – either the man himself or his parents. Likewise today there is a lot of blame in religion, especially in Christianity. There is a lot of guilt. I have heard Christianity called a guilt management system. It is not just Christianity. The Indian idea of karma and reincarnation blames a person's present condition on past conduct in previous lives. That is just a variation of the "blame the victim" game.

Guilt is a psychological obstacle to spiritual realization. Jesus does not hesitate to undermine the disciples attempt to impose a guilt trip on the man or his parents. Jesus answered, "It was neither that this man sinned, nor his parents; but it was so that the works of God might be displayed in him." Jesus says it is was not this man's fault that he was born blind. Likewise it is not our fault when we cannot spiritually see the Kingdom of God. Jesus says we need to stop dwelling on the past and see the opportunity in the present. He says, "It was so that the works of God might be displayed in him."

The Buddha said a similar thing when people came to him wanting to know the reason for human suffering. He said that question was like a man being struck with an arrow and wanting to know all about the arrow. What kind of wood it was made of, what kind of feathers were on it, what type of bow was used to shoot it, who shot it and why, etc. Buddha said, "Forget all that! Just take the arrow out!" That was the Buddha's way of cutting through the theoretical and getting to the practical.

Jesus says that the solution to the man's

blindness is "I AM." Jesus gives one of his I AM statements here. He says, "While I am in the world, I am the Light of the world." In the previous chapter Jesus had said, "I am the light of the world. Whoever follows me will never walk in darkness, but will have the light of life." I AM statements, as I have said before in this book, are about Jesus' eternal nature and identity and our eternal nature and identity. Here Jesus says he is the light of the world. In the Sermon on the Mount Jesus said, "You are the Light of the world. ... let your light shine." Christ's true nature and our true nature is the cure for spiritual blindness.

The next issue that Jesus deals with is spiritual practice. That is another obstacle to spiritual sight. People feel like they need to do something in order to be able to spiritually see what Jesus could see. The same today. Christians think they have to follow a bunch of moral laws or believe a bunch of theological doctrines. Or they need to spend more time in prayer and Bible Reading. In Eastern spiritual traditions they think they need to practice the right spiritual disciplines or have the right spiritual teacher or meditate using the right technique. Religious people do all these things earnestly and then wonder why they don't work.

Some people believe in the efficacy of techniques. Apparently the man in the story did. So that is what Jesus gives him. Jesus spit on the ground, made mud from the saliva, applied the mud to the man's eyes, and said to him, "Go, wash in the pool of Siloam." So the man did as he was told. He left and washed, and came back seeing. Jesus didn't need to do those things, and neither did the man. Jesus had done many other healings without any such theatrics. It was not about magic mud or sacred spit or holy water. It was about the Light of the World.

When it comes to spiritual awakening, it is not

about techniques or spiritual practices. When it comes to salvation it is not about beliefs or morality. It is about spiritual identity. That is why this story moves the focus from healing to the identity of Jesus. The rest of the chapter is about religious leaders questioning the man about who healed him and who exactly Jesus is. The answer is already given before the miracle happened. "I am the Light of the World."

The man ends up becoming a follower of Jesus. We are told that the religious leaders decided to excommunicate any followers of Jesus from the synagogue. This is the way traditional religious leaders deal with dissent. They are threatened by anything that does not fit in their religious box. Jesus has a discussion about this with the religious leaders. Jesus said, "For judgment I came into this world, so that those who do not see may see, and those who see may become blind." The Pharisees said to Him, "We are blind then?" Jesus said to them, "If you were blind, you would have no sin; but now that you maintain, 'We see,' your sin remains."

This is an indictment of traditional religion, which is represented by the Pharisees in this story. Today we might call it the institutional church or organized religion. These are religious people who are convinced they have it all figured out. They believe they have the truth and anyone who thinks otherwise is lost, a blasphemer, or a heretic. This kind of closemindedness is the greatest obstacle to spiritual sight.

Such spiritual pride and arrogance keep people from seeing the Kingdom of God. I see in my own religion of Christianity, especially in more rigid forms of it, such as fundamentalism, evangelicalism and other conservative forms of Christianity. Liberal and progressive Christians can also be closeminded in their own way. Like the Pharisees the spiritually arrogant say, "We see," yet according to Jesus they are blind. As the Tao Te Ching says, "Those who speak do not know. Those who know do not speak."

So where does that leave the spiritual seeker today? It leaves us with grace. Grace frees us from guilt. Guilt and shame are spiritual poison. I recommend that people run from any religious leader that piles on guilt, and then says they can provide you the cure for your guilt. They are spiritual snake oil salesmen. And we all know who the snake is in the Bible. Your present spiritual condition is not your fault, so don't beat yourself up any longer.

When it comes to spiritual practices, there is nothing you can do or not do that will make a difference. It is all grace. That is not permission to abandon the spiritual path. Go ahead and continue the spiritual disciplines that seem meaningful, but relax. Practice is more about intention than intensity. Simply rest in the grace of God. It is not about doing the right things the right way. It is not about belonging to the right group or holding the right beliefs.

It is about spiritual identity: Christ's identity and our identity. That is what this story teaches. When we see what we are, we see who Christ is and God is. That is awakening. That is Self-realization. We see that Jesus is the Light of the world and that we are the Light of the world. We see everything else in that light. We see the world as it is and not as the illusion it appears to be. We see Reality. That is what it means to see the Kingdom of God and to enter the Kingdom of God.

There is no trick to seeing this. The truth is everyone already sees this at some level. This is who we are. It is just that we have ignored it, which is what ignorance means. The Pharisees knew this at some level, but they refused to see it. That is why Jesus called them willfully spiritually blind. Elsewhere he calls them the blind leading the blind.

Jesus came into the world so that all may see. That was his mission. "I came into this world, so that those who do not see may see, and those who see may become blind." He came that we might see that we are the light of the world by which the world sees.

LIFE ABUNDANT AND ETERNAL

The Parable of the Sheepfold is a metaphor for Nondual Reality. Jesus tells us how to enter into unitive awareness, which he calls Life Abundant and Eternal Life. The story is undoubtedly drawn from his own experience growing up in Galilee. The Gospels say that Jesus was a carpenter, but I wonder if he had friends or family in Nazareth who were shepherds. Perhaps the young Jesus went with these shepherds into the fields on occasion to tend the sheep. He certainly knows a lot about shepherds and sheep, and he uses them often in his teachings. He even calls himself "the good shepherd" in our story. He never calls himself "the good carpenter."

In chapter 10 of the Gospel of John Jesus describes a sheepfold that shepherds would have used when they had to spend the night outdoors with their sheep. It was not like the scene on Christmas cards with stars shining and sheep scattered across the fields. If that were the case they would have lost sheep to predators or wandering off during the night. Shepherds kept sheep in a sheepfold at night. Sheepfolds were enclosures made of stone walls, much like the stone walls that are everywhere in New Hampshire, including around the perimeter of my property.

When I first visited Israel in 1983 I remember thinking that these sheepfolds looked exactly like the town pound just down the street from my house in New Hampshire. It was built in the 1770's to house stray animals. It is not used for that purpose any longer, but it is preserved for historical purposes and has a sign identifying it. It is just a square stone enclosure with a gate. That is the way sheepfolds were in Palestine.

Along with this parable of the sheepfold Jesus gives three I AM statements in chapter 10, as well as a couple other famous sayings. He says "I am the gate [or the door] to the sheepfold." He says, "I am the Good Shepherd." Finally he says bluntly "I am the Son of God." He also gives two other famous sayings: "I came so that they would have life, and have it abundantly" and "I and the Father are one."

The sheepfold represents the Kingdom of God, which I call unitive awareness. He is talking about how to enter into this nondual awareness. The only way to enter into this awareness is through him. "Truly, truly I say to you, the one who does not enter by the door into the fold of the sheep, but climbs up some other way, he is a thief and a robber." Then he says, "I am the door; if anyone enters through me, he will be saved, and will go in and out and find pasture."

Jesus is speaking here - and everywhere in this Gospel - as the Eternal One, the Divine I AM. He is not saying that you have to be a Christian to enter the sheepfold. Jesus makes that clear when he says, "I have other sheep that are not of this fold; I must bring them also, and they will listen to my voice; and they will become one flock, with one shepherd." He is referring to people of other religions. All faiths are part of his sheepfold, but they all have to come through the I AM. That is why he has more I AM sayings here than any other chapter. To come into the Kingdom of God we come through that nondual awareness known as I AM.

That is what he means when he says "I am the good shepherd." The shepherd was literally the door to the sheepfold. When the shepherd spent the night in the fields, the shepherd would lie down across the entrance to the sheepfold. He literally became the gate to the sheepfold. Nothing was getting in or out without going through him.

Several times Jesus make reference to his role as the shepherd saying, "I lay down My life for the sheep." The door to unitive awareness is through laying down one's life. It means the death of the self in order to enter into the bigger identity of the I AM. That is what the Cross is about as well. It is a proclamation that the way to Eternal Life is through the death of the personal individual self.

This parable of the sheepfold contains echoes of the Garden of Eden, which is pictured in Genesis as a walled garden with an entrance at the east, just like the temple in Jerusalem. The temple was a symbolic Garden of Eden. Eden represents Nondual Reality before humans developed a sense of separation. In the Eden story, Adam and Eve were cast out of the garden after they became self-aware.

Genesis says a cherub with a flaming sword stood guard at the entrance to the garden to prevent anyone from entering the garden and eating of the Tree of Life and living forever. The cherub was the gate. To get into Eden you have to go through him, which means you have to die. You have to lay down your life. Jesus is being an example to us that we are to lay down our lives, just as he lay down his life, if we are to enter the sheepfold of the Kingdom of God.

When one contemplates the symbol of a walled sheepfold or garden, it may appear to be the antithesis of nonduality. Walls represent dualism,

THE GOSPEL OF NONDUALITY

not nondualism. As Robert Frost writes, "Before I built a wall I'd ask to know / What I was walling in or walling out." Then we hear the rest of Jesus' words: "I am the door; if anyone enters through Me, he will be saved, and will go in and out and find pasture." The wall is breached by the door. There is a passage from duality to nonduality. We go in and out. In other words the gate is open. Just like the New Jerusalem in the Book of Revelation, the doors to the Kingdom of God always stand open. This is describing the openness and spaciousness of nondual reality.

I was on a Zoom talk recently with a group of Christians that was studying one of my books. We were talking about the sense of self, and a woman remarked that she felt like she was in her body. She asked what I experienced. I replied that I experienced the body as in me. I was being quite honest. I no longer think of myself as localized inside a body. The body is here, but it is not me and I am not in it. I am not going to cease to be when the body is gone. Jesus said, "I give them eternal life, and they will never perish."

Some people talk about God being in us. That is true, but it is only half of the truth. Jesus says, "The Father is in me, and I in the Father." God is in me, but I am also in God. The boundary is porous. The gate is open and we go in and out. We are not contained by boundaries. This is what Jesus called abundant life. "I came so that they would have life, and have it abundantly." Abundant means overflowing containers and boundaries. My cup runneth over. There are no limits to Eternal Life.

After Jesus tells this parable he gets into an argument with the Pharisees. They have actually picked up stones and are about to stone him for blasphemy, because he said "I and the Father are one." When asked by Jesus why they are stoning him they said, "We are not stoning You for a good work, but for blasphemy; and because you, being a man, make yourself out to be God."

Then Jesus gave the most startling statement he has ever made. Jesus quoted from the Hebrew Bible. "Has it not been written in your Law: 'I said, you are gods'? If he called them gods, to whom the word of God came (and the Scripture cannot be nullified), are you saying of him whom the Father sanctified and sent into the world, 'You are blaspheming,' because I said, 'I am the Son of God'?

Jesus was quoting Psalm 82. This Old Testament passage actually says something much more controversial In Hebrew than in the New Testament Greek. It says to humans, "You are Elohim," which is the most common Hebrew word for God. It was saying, and Jesus was saying, that humans are one with God, just like Jesus was claiming to be one with God. He quoted this "so that you may know and understand that the Father is in me, and I in the Father."

Jesus is talking about our identity with the Divine. That is the I AM Awareness. Jesus tells the parable of the sheepfold to teach people about his true nature and our true nature. Jesus was successful in getting across this message. They understood it, but they did not like it. They thought it was blasphemy and wanted to get rid of both the message and the messenger. Things have not changed. Traditional Christianity still calls this blasphemy and want to get rid of the teaching and those who teach it. This is what I am teaching. This is Eternal Life. This is life abundant and eternal. Jesus said, "I came so that they would have life, and have it abundantly." This life is yours. It is who you are.

HOW TO NOT DIE

We all have to deal with death sooner or later. If you read the newspaper you face this reality every day. George Burns said, "I wake up every morning and read the morning newspaper. I look at the obituaries, and if my name is not there, I eat breakfast." This morning I read the local paper and scanned the obituaries. There were seven of them. The deceased were ages 71, 78, 64, 90, 71, 28 and 68. Those ages are uncomfortably close to my own age of 70. When you approach the average life expectancy, you realize more clearly that one day you are going to die.

As I write these words COVID is sweeping through the nation, and we are even more conscious of the possibility of dying. As I am writing this, 3000 Americans are dying every day of this virus. Every day the death toll exceeds the causalities of Pearl Harbor or 9/11.

We all die. The mortality rate is still 100%, regardless of what your Sunday School teacher or preacher told you about Elijah and Enoch, two people in the Bible who traditionally are said not to have died. They died. The biblical depictions of their departure are just metaphors for dying. Also there is not going to be a rapture that allows a certain generation of lucky Christians to avoid death. That idea was created by some crazy Christians in the 19th century. It ain't gonna happen. Everything that is born dies. That is the nature of this physical realm.

Thank God for death. It inspires us to search for that which does not die. If we did not die, we would never search for the eternal. At this point I need to amend what I just said about everybody dying. I mean that every body dies. The body dies. If we identify with the body, then we imagine we will die with it. If we are a little human consciousness that resides in a body – like the old-time idea of a homunculus - then we would die when the brain dies.

The truth is we are not the body, nor are we the personality that seems to reside within the body. Salvation - or spiritual awakening or enlightenment – is waking up to what we really are, which cannot die. What we really are is not born and does not die. This is obvious when we see our identity as Being Itself rather than a human being.

Many people who have Near Death experiences – who die for a few minutes and are resuscitated and have stories to tell of what happened while they were dead – lose their fear of death. The last funeral I conducted was for a friend of mine – younger than me, by the way – who had a Near Death experience and told me about it. She had no fear of death afterwards.

Spiritual awakening is like this. It conquers the fear of death. That is what the famous story of Jesus raising Lazarus from the dead is all about. It is found in the eleventh chapter of the Gospel of John. The story is about how three different people – Mary, Martha, and Jesus - deal with death. Mary and Martha were the sisters of Jesus' friend Lazarus.

Lazarus became seriously ill, and his sisters called for Jesus to come to heal him. Lazarus was one of Jesus' best friends. Surely he would come and save his life, they thought. He did not. When Jesus got the message, he waited two more days, until he heard that Lazarus was dead. By the time Jesus arrived, Lazarus had been in the grave for four days. To emphasize the point that Lazarus was really dead, the story tells us that his body was already stinking. This was not a near death experience. This was a real death experience.

Jesus met with the two sisters. They both expressed anger at him for not coming sooner, when he could have prevented Lazarus' death. It is a very emotional chapter. Not only are the sisters emotional, it says that Jesus was moved deeply and wept. Being one with God doesn't mean we do not cry or grieve. Jesus grieved.

There is a story about the Taoist master Chuang Tzu. His beloved wife of many years died. When his best friend came to his house to mourn with him, he found him sitting on the floor with an inverted bowl on his knees, drumming on it and singing. The friend scolded Chuang Tzu for not showing proper respect. Chuang Tzu replied that when his wife died, he initially grieved greatly because he loved her deeply. Then he remembered that she had returned to what she was before she was born. So he sat down and sang a song of joy.

When Jesus' friend Lazarus died, Jesus wept. Then he remembered who he was and who Lazarus was. In the story Jesus communicated this reality both in words and in symbolic action by raising him from the dead. Remember that this is a story. This tale is not meant to be taken literally as history or science. That is the way literalists and fundamentalists will read this passage, but there are other ways to interpret scripture. This is a symbolic story meant to communicate spiritual truth. That truth is found in the statement Jesus makes.

Jesus tells the sisters that Lazarus will rise again. They both say that they believe that he will rise again at the last day. Jesus says he is not talking about a future Resurrection Day. He is talking about a living reality here and now. Jesus said, "I am the resurrection and the life; the one who believes in Me will live, even if he dies, and everyone who lives and believes in Me will never die." Jesus is saying that Lazarus lives even though he is dead, and the sisters will never die.

Jesus said, "Everyone who lives and believes in me will never die." He is obviously not talking about physical death of the body here. We all physically die. Lazarus died physically. Jesus died physically. He is talking about spiritual life – eternal life. For Jesus resurrection is not about an event some day in the future. It is about now. "I AM the resurrection and the Life."

Whether or not there is a physical body, we are Life. Jesus no longer has a physical body now but he is still the Resurrection and the Life. That is the reality that Jesus is communicating. This gospel story is not about a mummy hopping out of a tomb and having to be unbound from its burial clothes. It is about us being unbound from our way of thinking about life and death.

Jesus said, "And everyone who lives and believes in me will never die." I will never die. I know it not only because I believe Jesus. I know it firsthand. That doesn't mean that this body will not die. It will. It does not mean that Marshall Davis will not cease to exist. That persona will cease. But what I am cannot not die, because I AM is not the body and was not born. I am one with the Eternal Christ and share Christ's divine life. It is the one life. That is Nonduality.

The good news – the gospel – is that this is knowable here and now for everyone. To be saved is not to hope for a reserved spot in heaven when we die, as long as we believe the right things and act the right way. It is to wake up to the Reality that Jesus called Eternal Life. We do not have to wait until we die to go to heaven. We do not have to wait for the resurrection day. Now is the Day of Salvation. Now is Eternal Life. I AM.

That is what Jesus was pointing to when he said, "I am the Resurrection and the Life." Resurrection is just another word for Eternal Life. Resurrection is being born again. It is Spiritual Awakening. Resurrection is Enlightenment. It is knowing Eternity now as our true nature and identity, just as it was Jesus' nature and identity.

"I am the resurrection and the life; the one who believes in Me will live, even though he dies, and everyone who lives and believes in Me will never die." To believe in Christ means being one with the Eternal Christ. This is union with God. We will never die because we are Life. Life cannot die. Though the body be in a grave, we do not die. That is the Resurrection and the Life.

JESUS IS MY GURU

The disciples of Jesus called him Rabbi, which means teacher. Jesus is my Rabbi. Jesus is my Lord. He is my Savior. He is the Christ. I am comfortable using all these traditional Christian terms, even though my mystical approach to Christianity is not the type you normally find at your neighborhood church.

In India they use the word Guru. Even though this term may sound strange to Christian ears, Jesus is my Guru. It is not important what word is used. It is important to have a spiritual teacher. Left to our own resources we can wander in the wilderness for forty years and never see the Promised Land.

Jesus is my spiritual teacher. A lot of other spiritual sages have helped me along the way. The Buddha has been very helpful. So has Lao Tzu, author of the Tao Te Ching and the Taoist teacher Chuang Tzu. The authors of the Upanishads have taught me a lot. Meister Eckhart has been important to me, as has Shankara.

I came of age in the 1960's and early 70's. Cultural icons like Alan Watts and Ram Dass were important to me at that time, as well as Mahatma Gandhi and Martin Luther King. Writers like Aldous

Huxley, Huston Smith, Thomas Merton, and Evelyn Underhill have helped. More recently Ramana Maharshi has illuminated the way, as well the writings of his disciples. I have learned from all of these, but Jesus is my Guru, my Teacher, my Lord, and my Savior. An icon of Christ hangs on my wall, not a photo of Ramana or an image of Buddha.

Jesus showed me the Kingdom of God. He led me into the Kingdom of God. He taught me that the Kingdom of God is within and around me. He has done that through his teachings written in the gospels, but more importantly by his Living Presence here and now. Even though Jesus died many centuries ago, as the Eternal Christ he is still present as he promised he would be. For that reason I unashamedly call myself a follower of Jesus Christ.

I see no contradiction between being a Christian and learning from these other spiritual teachers. It is the same gospel being proclaimed. Many Christians disagree with this assessment. They see religion as a zero-sum game - another religion's gains are Christianity's losses. Christians compete with other religions to win souls for their team, and they rejoice when a Muslim or a Hindu becomes a Christian. That has traditionally been the purpose of Christian missions.

I see all religions as variations on the one eternal gospel, the perennial philosophy. As a Christian pastor I am not in competition with other faiths. We are on the same team. Yet I unapologetically call myself a Christian. I follow the teachings of Christ, who is alive and present today.

In the twelfth chapter of the Gospel of John, we see the transition from an emphasis on the teachings of Christ to an emphasis on the life of Christ, in particular the final week of Jesus' life. We learn from his life as well as his words.

Chapter twelve opens with Palm Sunday, and the

rest of the book brings us through Easter Sunday and beyond. In this chapter Jesus comments on this shift. He says, "The hour has come for the Son of Man to be glorified. Truly, truly I say to you, unless a grain of wheat falls into the earth and dies, it remains alone; but if it dies, it bears much fruit." This was Jesus' way of saying that his death was necessary to move the gospel to the next level.

Christ was one Jewish man living in first century Palestine, and his ministry and teachings were limited to that setting. But with his death and glorification, his ministry expanded to all times and places. Jesus says, "And I, if I am lifted up from the earth, will draw all people to Myself." The death of Jesus was not an unfortunate tragedy or a mistake. It was an intentional strategy to expand his ministry beyond his lifespan.

In this chapter the words "glory" and "glorify" are used to describe this transition. Jesus is struggling with the emotional aspect of dying. After all, he was a human with human feelings. He says, "Now My soul has become troubled. What am I to say? 'Father, save Me from this hour'? But for this purpose I came to this hour. Father, glorify Your name." Then a voice came out of heaven: "I have both glorified it, and will glorify it again."

When one has Jesus as one's spiritual teacher it is as if we were living in the first century in Palestine. Sometimes I hear Christians pining for the old days – the biblical times - and wishing they could have heard Jesus teach with their own ears. We can! It is even better now than then, for Christ is within us.

That is the important thing to remember about a spiritual teacher. Regardless of what human teacher we might have, there is only one real Teacher. That teacher is within. That teacher is the True Self, the Inner Christ. The human teacher is only useful to direct our attention to the Teacher that resides within. In that way the Teacher is with us always and never leaves us.

The crowd of people who had gathered for Palm Sunday says to Jesus: "We have heard from the Law that the Christ is to remain forever; and how is it that You say, 'The Son of Man must be lifted up'? Who is this Son of Man?" So Jesus said to them, "For a little while longer the Light is among you. Walk while you have the Light, so that darkness will not overtake you; also, the one who walks in the darkness does not know where he is going. While you have the Light, believe in the Light, so that you may become sons of Light."

Jesus is speaking about his forthcoming death, which he compares to darkness falling. His words reprise the theme found in the prologue of the Gospel of John, which I call John's Christmas poem. The prologue says that light was coming into the world in Jesus. It says the light shines in the darkness and the darkness has not put it out. I put that verse on our Christmas cards this year. Not even the execution of Jesus was able to extinguish the Light. That is because Jesus taught us to be sons and daughters of the Light. We are the light of the world.

The Light that shines in the darkness shines within us. The Teacher is within. Human teachers come and go. They are born and they die. The Eternal Teacher is not born and does not die. This Teacher does not come and go. This teacher is always present. Good spiritual teachers point us to that one Teacher. They do not desire to be worshipped or served. A true teacher points to the Teacher within. True teachers work themselves out of a job.

That is why it is alright when they die. Death is just another opportunity to teach that the real teacher does not die. That is the meaning of the resurrection of Jesus. The resurrection of Jesus is a dramatic way of depicting the truth that the Teacher cannot die – not really. The teacher's body can die, but the Teacher does not die. As Christ promised after the resurrection, "I am with you always, even unto the end of the age."

Without some type of spiritual director or spiritual guide to point us in the right direction, we are at the mercy of our body and mind. Our ego will pull us in all sorts of directions. The ego – the false self – will do anything to deceive us in order to remain in control of our lives. Left to our own resources we deceive ourselves. That is why it is important to have someone to show the way. It is the same reason that counselors and therapists are helpful to guide us to psychological health. We need someone who is spiritually mature enough to direct us to the Teacher within.

Human teachers are not perfect, and we must not mistake them for such. If we deify them, they will disappoint us. But if we find a genuine teacher, they are useful to point us to the One who is perfect. But be careful. There are a lot of spiritual con men and greedy gurus out there. There are so-called spiritual teachers who use their position to feed the ego and the body. As Jesus said, "You will know them by their fruits.

All true spiritual teachers throughout the ages in all the different spiritual traditions are in essence the same Spiritual Teacher. Jesus called his inner Teacher "the Father." "For I did not speak on My own, but the Father Himself who sent Me has given Me ... what to say and what to speak. The things I speak, I speak just as the Father has told Me." There is only One Teacher speaking through human teachers. It is just a matter of recognizing this voice and following this teacher. I call this inner teacher Jesus Christ.

A NONDUAL SACRAMENT

I speak about Christian nonduality. People ask why I use that term, and not just nonduality. After all, the adjective "Christian" seems to make it dualistic, distinguishing it from other types of nonduality, as if such a thing were possible. What I mean by "Christian nonduality" is the nonduality taught by Christ and expressed in Christian terms. There is a unique flavor to Christian nonduality. Just as Himalayan salt has a distinctive pink tint to it, so does Christian nonduality have a distinctive tint. It is the tint of love, a divine love which in the Greek Testament is called agape.

Love is present in other religions as well. The Buddhist virtue of compassion comes to mind. So it is really more a matter of emphasis. As I have studied the religions of the world, it seems that Christ emphasized love more than other religious teachers. In John 13 we have the picture of Christ on his knees with a towel wrapped around his waist washing his disciples' feet. This towel ceremony is what I am calling the sacrament of Christian nonduality.

In Protestant churches the term sacrament is reserved for the Lord's Supper and baptism. But in the Gospel of John both of those rites are downplayed. There is no institution of the Lord's Supper in John's gospel, and baptism is mentioned only in passing. Those rites are not given the prominence they have in the other three gospels. That is intentional. The spiritual community that developed around the apostle John in Ephesus was nonsacramental and nondual.

A Last Supper is mentioned but it is not a Passover Meal nor is it the Lord's Supper. In place of a sacrament of bread and wine we have another ritual mentioned – foot-washing. During the supper Jesus "got up from supper and laid His outer garments aside; and He took a towel and tied it around Himself. Then He poured water into the basin, and began washing the disciples' feet and wiping them with the towel which He had tied around Himself."

This is done during the meal, indicating its prominent position in the story. It takes the place of the Eucharist in John's depiction of the Last Supper. Normally foot-washing would be done as soon as one entered the door of the house. If it was a wealthy home, foot-washing would be done by a servant. In this case each guest would have been done it themselves. We can assume this is what happened, even though it is not mentioned.

Foot-washing was done because people reclined at the table with their feet off to one side. It is not too appetizing to eat a meal while smelling the dirty feet of your neighbor! So people took off their sandals and washed the dirt off their feet before they entered the room to eat. It is similar to the mud rooms we have in New Hampshire, where we take off our boots or shoes before entering a home.

The foot-washing ceremony instituted by Jesus was probably a second washing – meant to be symbolic. Jesus was playing the symbolic role of a servant. Sometimes a rabbi would have his feet washed by his disciples as a sign of respect and subservience. It was never the other way around. That is why Peter is so flustered by Jesus' action, and initially refuses to allow Jesus to wash his feet. It does not fit the traditional idea of the teacher-disciple relationship. But there was nothing traditional about Jesus' servant leadership.

After Jesus had gone around the table and washed all his disciples' feet, he put his robe back on. He "reclined at the table again, and He said to them, "Do you know what I have done for you? You call Me 'Teacher' and 'Lord'; and you are correct, for so I am. So if I, the Lord and the Teacher, washed your feet, you also ought to wash one another's feet. For I gave you an example, so that you also would do just as I did for you. Truly, truly I say to you, a slave is not greater than his master, nor is one who is sent greater than the one who sent him. If you know these things, you are blessed if you do them."

This is a sacrament of humility and service. It communicates egalitarianism, not hierarchy, which is very different than what the church embraced a few centuries later. This is a much more fitting sacrament for nonduality: all are one. It as similar to the Eastern gesture of folding one's hands and bowing to people. That has become my alternative to shaking hands during this pandemic. In the East it is understood as God in me recognizing and bowing to God in you. "The Christ in Me Greets the Christ in Thee," is an old Christian greeting. There is a beautiful hymn: "Oh what a mystery! Christ in you, Christ in me! Oh what a victory! Christ in you, Christ in me!"

To make it clear exactly what the ritual was communicating, Jesus said to them, "I am giving you a new commandment, that you love one another; just as I have loved you, that you also love one another.

By this all people will know that you are My disciples: if you have love for one another."

According to Jesus love is the distinguishing mark of his disciples. He calls it a new commandment, which may seem odd. Didn't Jesus teach love previously? Yes. He taught that the greatest commandment was to love God with all one's heart. He said the second greatest commandment was to love our neighbor as ourselves. So how is this commandment new?

It is new because we are to love each other as Christ loves us. We are to follow the example of Christ. This is more than outward imitation. It is the love of Christ embodied in us. This is the incarnation of love. It is what Christmas is about. As the hymn says, "Love came down at Christmas."

This is what the Cross represents. The Cross is the embodiment of self-giving love. As Jesus says a couple of chapters later: "Greater love hath no man than this, that a man lay down his life for his friends." The sacrament of the towel foreshadows Jesus giving his life. Jesus calls this glory. "Now is the Son of Man glorified, and God is glorified in Him."

The glory is oneness. We are one with each other, one with Christ, and one with God. We can describe this oneness in theological and philosophical language, but that seems to take us further away from the reality of it. We are one. That is glory. In loving one another we are loving ourselves, which is the reality behind the command to love our neighbors as ourselves. This is also the meaning of loving God with all our heart, mind, soul and strength. When we love God, we are also loving ourselves because we are one with God.

Oneness is symbolized by the sacrament of the towel. Most people do feel the full impact of this story. In the middle of the meal Jesus took off his robe, which means his clothes. He stripped down to the first century equivalent of his underwear. He is wearing exactly what he would wear a short time later on the cross. While half naked he tied a long towel around his waist and washed his disciples' feet one by one. Imagine how long it would have taken to wash twelve sets of feet. Imagine the silence of the twelve disciples, including Judas who was about to betray him. This was a holy moment.

This sacrament is the embodiment of divine love. Not only love of our neighbor but love of our enemy. Judas Iscariot plays a prominent role in John's account of the Last Supper. Jesus was showing us what it means to love our enemies.

Christ in me serves the Christ in you in selfless love, because there is no self in love. This is a powerful ritual that acknowledges that we love God by loving our fellow humans with all our hearts, minds, soul and strength. This is because our fellow humans are one in God. This is Christian nonduality. This is wholehearted love based on the realization that all is one.

IS JESUS THE ONLY WAY?

In this chapter I address the issue faced by Christians when they come in contact with other faith traditions. Especially when they get to know people of other faiths and read the scriptures of non-Christian religions with an open mind. The question is this: Is Jesus Christ the only way to salvation? Framed another way, "Do you have to believe in Jesus to be saved?"

The traditional Christian answer is "Yes." The Catechism of the Catholic Church puts it this way: Outside the Church there is no salvation. Evangelicals point to certain passages of Scripture, especially two verses. One is in the Book of Acts where Peter is reported to have said, "Salvation exists in no one else, for there is no other name under heaven given to men by which we must be saved." Then there are the famous words of Jesus himself, "I am the way, the truth, and the life; no one comes to the Father except through Me." As the old fundamentalist slogan goes, "The Bible says it, I believe it, and that settles it"

I say, "Not so fast. Let's look at what Jesus really says." What is the context of these verses? This famous saying in the 14th chapter of the Gospel of

John is part of the farewell address that Jesus gives to his disciples the night before he dies. The sermon stretches for several chapters, but these words are found near the beginning.

Before it are words often spoken at funerals: "Let not your heart be troubled; you believe in God, believe also in Me. In My Father's house are many mansions; if it were not so, I would have told you. I go to prepare a place for you. And if I go and prepare a place for you, I will come again and receive you to Myself; that where I am, there you may be also."

Harvey Cox, the famous theologian of Harvard Divinity School, wrote a book in 1988 entitled "Many Mansions: A Christian's Encounter with Other Faiths." In that book he says the phrase "many mansions" refers to the different religions of the world. A few chapters back Jesus referred to having sheep who are not of this fold, referring to people of other faiths.

We see Jesus praising people of other faiths constantly. He refers to the faith of a Roman centurion, who was not a Jew or a Christian, saying, "Truly I tell you, I have not found anyone in Israel with such great faith. I say to you that many will come from the east and the west to share the banquet with Abraham, Isaac, and Jacob in the kingdom of heaven." Jesus is clearly saying that not just Jews will enter the Kingdom of God.

We saw the same thing with the Samaritan woman at the well. It was the meaning of the visit of the Magi to the Christ child. It is present in the stories of the Syro-Phoenician woman (also called Canaanite woman), the Samaritan leper, as well as Jesus' encounters with people from the Decapolis who were not Jewish. Then there is his famous parable of the Good Samaritan. These are not just people of different ethnic heritage; these were people of different religious faiths. That aspect of the stories is routinely ignored by Christian preachers.

Jesus is continually using people of other faiths as examples of godly persons. One's cultural tradition – including one's religious beliefs and practices - did not matter at all to Jesus. What did matter was that people could see beyond the confines of their own religion. It was the self-righteous people of his own religion that Jesus called children of the devil, and he said they would not enter the Kingdom of God. Jesus did not mince words when dealing with people who excluded others for religious reasons.

When we look at the whole testimony of Jesus, and not just pluck verses out of context to shore up our own religious prejudices, then we see that declaring himself to be "the way, the truth and the life" has nothing to do with religious systems. When Jesus said, "no one comes to the Father except through Me" he was not trumpeting his religion over others. He was not excluding non-Christians from the Kingdom of Heaven. If he had been, he would have been no better than the Pharisees.

Then what was he saying? We need to always remember that when Jesus speaks in the Gospel of John, he is speaking as the Eternal Logos. In the opening words of the Gospel we are told that Jesus is the Eternal Word who is God. That is who is speaking in all the I AM sayings. This is not one human being elevating himself above others. That would have been very unchristlike. Jesus just finished washing his disciples' feet to demonstrate the opposite of that. This is the Eternal Word saying that you have to come through his eternal identity as the I AM to know God.

That becomes clear when we read the rest of his statement and not cut him off in mid thought. After Jesus says he is "the Way, the Truth and the Life," he takes a breath and says, "If you had known Me, you would have known My Father also; from now on you know Him, and have seen Him." This is a variation on Jesus' statement that he and the Father are one. If you know one, you know the other. Jesus is saying that he is identical with God.

Jesus gets into a conversation with his disciple Philip at this point. Jesus says to him, "I am in the Father, and the Father is in Me. The words that I say to you I do not speak on My own, but the Father, as He abides in Me, does His works. Believe Me that I am in the Father and the Father is in Me."

This leads Jesus to talk about the Holy Spirit. He continues, "I will ask the Father, and He will give you another Helper [Comforter, Counselor], so that He may be with you forever; the Helper is the Spirit of truth, whom the world cannot receive, because it does not see Him or know Him; but you know Him because He remains with you and will be in you."

Jesus talks about himself, the Holy Spirit and the Father. So this is probably a good time to say a word about the Trinity. This is not the complex theological doctrine that came centuries later. Here Jesus is simply using different words for the Divine. Put simply, the Father is Divine transcendence. The Spirit is Divine immanence. And the Son is divine incarnation - the experience of God incarnated a human being.

That is an oversimplification of course. Each of those terms shares aspects of the others. For example he also says the Father is in him, so the Father is an inner presence also. In any case these three are one. That is the trinity. They are one God, nondual. The Father is the Spirit. Transcendence is immanence. Brahman is Atman. This is our nature as human incarnation. The Son – which Jesus refers to as both the Son of God and the Son of Man – is both divine and human. Two are one. That thou art.

Jesus mentions the coming of the Holy Spirit and the Second Coming. Those two are also one. Jesus says, "I am going away, and I am coming to you." The Holy Spirt is called the Spirit of Jesus elsewhere in the New Testament. In the synoptic Gospels as the Pauline writings, the Second Coming is interpreted as a personal physical return of the man Jesus. But that is not the case in the Gospel of John. In chapter 14 Jesus says that he is going away, but he returns in the resurrection and the Spirit.

In the Gospel of John, the Coming of the Holy Spirit and the Second Coming occur immediately after the resurrection of Jesus. In chapter 20 the risen Christ breathes on the disciples and says to them, "Receive the Holy Spirit." This is known by scholars as the Johannine Pentecost. The author of the Gospel of John is reinterpreting both the Second Coming and Pentecost as the presence of God with us and in us.

In the Gospel of John, the Coming of the Holy Spirit and the Second Coming of Christ are fulfilled when we are united with the Father and Christ in the Spirit. This he calls divine peace, "Peace I leave you, My peace I give you; not as the world gives, do I give to you." John's Gospel is truly nondualistic in a way that the other gospels are not.

Now let's return to the original question posed by this chapter: Is Jesus Christ the only way? If that means "Do you have to be a Christian to enter the Kingdom of God?" the answer is no. The Kingdom is bigger than any single religion. As Jesus said after praising the faith of the Roman centurion, "I say to you that many will come from the east and the west to share the banquet with Abraham, Isaac, and Jacob in the kingdom of heaven." That is the Way, the Truth and the Life. Many religions, one Truth.

But if one sees Jesus speaking these words as the Eternal Logos, the answer is Yes. It is only through the Eternal I AM that anyone of any religion enters the Kingdom of God. I AM is the Eternal Name of

Christ. "For there is no other name under heaven given to men by which we must be saved." That is the strait gate and narrow way.

When Jesus says "I am the Way, the Truth and the Life," he means the narrow way of I AM. Not the narrow-minded way of "I am this" or "I am that" that we find in religious fundamentalism. The Way is not propositional Truth found in doctrines. I AM is strait and narrow in a spiritual sense. The only way to squeeze through that narrow gate is to shed one's ego including egoic religion – to shed one's human self until we are no more, and there is only God. When there is only I AM, that is the Realm of God. That is the Kingdom of Heaven.

ABIDING IN UNITIVE AWARENESS

The further we travel into the Gospel of John, the closer we come to the core of John's gospel of nonduality. The structure of the gospel up to this point has been seven signs of Jesus, accompanied by seven teachings of Jesus, which include seven I AM sayings. In the 15th chapter we have the last of these sayings. Jesus says, "I am the true vine, and My Father is the vinedresser." A couple of verses later he adds, "I am the vine, you are the branches."

In fleshing out this metaphor Jesus talks about "abiding." Some translations use the word remain or dwell, but I prefer the word "abide" because it means to make one's home in, as in the word abode. It means to live in. Jesus says, "Abide in Me, and I in you." This is my awareness of Christ. I abide I Christ and Christ in me.

In our local newspaper there is a weekly religious column written by an evangelical and political conservative. His most recent article was entitled "Turned off by Religion." In the article the author repeated the evangelical mantra, "It is not about religion. It is about relationship – a relationship with Jesus Christ." When I hear that I respond, "It is not about religion or relationship. It is about reality."

A relationship with God and Christ is good. But as the saying goes, "The good is the enemy of the best." I was an evangelical for decades, so I know all about having a personal relationship with Jesus. Then I went beyond relationship and discovered the best. A relationship is by nature dualistic. To be a relationship there has to be at least two. But in reality there is one – nondual.

Devotional religion is based on dualistic relationship with a separate God, and that is fine as far as it goes. But there is more to spirituality than relationship with God understood as a divine person. There is the experiential Reality of nonduality. This is not about religion or relationship; it is about identity – identity with God where two become one. Jesus expressed it as "I and the Father are one." This awareness is a quantum leap beyond traditional Christianity. This is union with God or "abiding in Christ."

A dualistic relationship with Christ is nothing compared to being one with Christ. In Christ we are united with God and all creation. In this union there is no distinction between us and not us. In unitive awareness the individual self, who is in relationship with God, ceases to exist. The boundaries dissolve and the self disappears. The self is seen as a psychological fiction, which means that its relationships are essentially fiction.

Instead there is only one. This can be called Reality, but there is really no good name for this. I use the word God, but this is not the theistic concept of God. Meister Eckhart calls this the God beyond God or the Godhead. It includes the personal God, but transcends the personal God to the same degree that the theistic God transcends an idol. Paul Tillich calls this Being Itself or the Ground of Being. This union is what we really yearn for when we desire a closer relationship with God.

The insufficiency of the evangelical gospel is why so many evangelicals end up leaving the fold and abandoning Christianity. This exodus from traditional Christianity has become an epidemic in recent years. If a relationship with Jesus was as fulfilling as evangelical preachers say it is, no one would ever abandon it. Yet there are growing numbers of deconversions to atheism and drop outs from the church by people who describe themselves as "spiritual but not religious." The politicizing of evangelical Christianity is only accelerating this trend. Christians are outgrowing evangelicalism.

There is an evangelical wannabe megachurch in our area, which I sometimes refer to as a starter church. It is a good place to get people started in Christianity, but it is elementary level spirituality. It is helpful for those who are beginning the spiritual life, but it can only bring people so far. When people start to grow, they end up leaving the church because that type of Christianity cannot bring them any further. It is like a child leaving home. This is a healthy thing. This church thinks these people are falling away or backsliding, but in fact they are outgrowing that type of Christianity.

Jesus says, "I am the true vine, and My Father is the vinedresser. Every branch in Me that does not bear fruit, He takes away; and every branch that bears fruit, He prunes it so that it may bear more fruit." God prunes our lives of dead religion. Dead wood has to be trimmed, and even good wood needs to be trimmed back to produce more fruit. Leaving Evangelicalism can be a painful experience, but it is necessary. Growth and fruitfulness demands pruning.

This process is called the Via Negativa. The negative way. It is the way of removing everything that is not God. One discovers True God by removing from one's life all forms of fake God. Like the layers of an onion, there are layers and layers of fake God in traditional religion. God peels back the layers from our lives and throws them away. God removes the idols. When the last layer is removed, nothing remains. Then we see that everything is God. I know that sounds contradictory, but it is real. God takes away everything, until nothing is left and what remains is God ... the True Self.

Spirituality is abiding in the True Self, which is called Christ. It is abiding in Christ. A healthy spirituality is not finished until this happens, until the ego is no more and one is united with God, where there is no separation between us and God. There are no boundaries between who we are, who God is, and what the universe is. All is one. This Reality is simply what is. This is unitive awareness, which spiritual traditions call liberation, awakening, enlightenment, satori, moksha, nirvana or a dozen other terms. It is oneness. Nondual awareness. Union with God.

This is what Jesus calls abiding in him. Jesus says, "Abide in Me, and I in you. Just as the branch cannot bear fruit of itself but must abide in the vine, so neither can you unless you abide in Me. I am the vine, you are the branches; the one who abides in Me, and I in him bears much fruit, for apart from Me you can do nothing." In reality there is no difference between the vine and the branches. You cannot tell where one ends and the other starts. They are one. So it is with God and us.

In the next verse Jesus says, "If anyone does not abide in Me, he is thrown away like a branch and dries up; and they gather them and throw them into the fire, and they are burned." That has traditionally been seen as a warning about being thrown into hell. But that is not what this means. This is not a threat. This is a promise. It is the destruction of ego. Everything that is not God must be cast off. Even

Paul knew this. In Philippians he lists everything about his previous life in dualistic religion. Then he says:

"But whatever things were gain to me, these things I have counted as loss because of Christ. More than that, I count all things loss in the surpassing greatness of knowing Christ Jesus my Lord, for whom I have suffered the loss of all things, and count them as rubbish, so that I may gain Christ, and may be found in Him...." The original text is actually stronger than that. The word translated "rubbish" actually means excrement. You heard me right. Paul used the S word from the pulpit. He flushed religion down the toilet in order to abide in Christ.

The spiritual life is a process of elimination – pun intended. We search for what we really are and what God really is. We examine our lives carefully and discard everything that that is not eternal. This is called Self-inquiry or God inquiry, depending on whether we are approaching the spiritual search by looking for God or looking for one's true self. It ends up at the same destination, but it can be approached from either side. In my case it was approached from both directions at once - like two teams digging a tunnel from opposite ends until they met in the center. When meeting in the center one comes face to face with one's true Self. At that moment of seeing, illusion falls away and one is face to face with reality.

Jesus describes the results of this union. He says, "You will abide in my love. These things I have spoken to you so that My joy may be in you, and that your joy may be made full." He also warns that there are other consequences to spiritual union, including persecution by worldly religious authorities who do not understand it and oppose it. He says, "If the world hates you, you know that it has hated Me before it hated you. If you were of the world, the world would love you as its own; but because you are not of the world ... the world hates you.... If they persecuted Me, they will persecute you as well.... All these things they will do to you on account of My name, because they do not know the One who sent Me."

The message of our essential oneness with God is not received by the institutional church. According to the Gospel of John, they are the ones that got Jesus executed on the charge of blasphemy. Jesus warns in the opening lines of the next chapter, "They will ban you from the congregation. An hour is coming when everyone who kills you will think that he is offering a service to God. These things they will do because they have not known the Father nor Me."

We should not be surprised if the gospel of nonduality is not received well by our evangelical friends or those in traditional mainline Christianity. This is the nature of the gospel. It is a stumbling block. This is the nature of Reality. It is the way it has to be. It is the way of the Cross. It is the way it will be until the Kingdom of God is realized on earth as it is in heaven.

A PRAYER OF NONDUALITY

In the 17th chapter of the Gospel of John we have one of the best descriptions of nonduality in the Bible. It occurs in the prayer offered by Jesus on the night he was arrested. The other three gospels set the final prayer of Jesus in the Garden of Gethsemane. There it is a prayer of agony. Jesus is sweating blood and asking God that he not die. Finally he surrenders to God's will. In John's gospel the prayer is very different. It occurs before they depart for the Mount of Olives. It is a prayer of inner peace describing unitive awareness.

This prayer can be broken into three parts. First Jesus prays for himself, then he prays for his disciples, and third he prays for future generations of disciples who would believe in him through the testimony of his disciples.

The theme of the first section is eternal life. The key word is glory. The word glory or glorify is used six times in five verses. Jesus begins by saying, "Father, the hour has come; glorify Your Son, so that the Son may glorify You." He ends the section by saying, "Father, glorify Me together with Yourself, with the glory which I had with You before the world existed."

He is talking about his departure from physical life to resume the glorious existence he had before he was born. This is a reference to this true nature as the Eternal Word, the Logos, the I AM, Being Itself. To be glorified is to return to that glory which he always was and is. To be glorified is to dwell in his true nature without a physical body.

This is glory for us as well. As we follow in the footsteps of Jesus we realize who we truly are, which is who Christ really is. That is why this is often called Self-realization. It is to experience what we were before birth and after death. It is to be fully aware of timeless nondual reality now.

The future dimension of eternal life is often emphasized by Christians. In popular Christianity this is pictured as going to heaven at death. As the gospel hymn says, "When all my labors and trials are o'er, And I am safe on that beautiful shore, Just to be near the dear Lord I adore Will through the ages be glory for me. Glory for me, glory for me! When by His grace I shall look on His face. That will be glory, be glory for me!"

Eternal life is pictured dualistically, which is the only way that the mind can conceive it. But the reality is nondual awareness. We are not just near the Lord and looking on his face, we are one with the Lord. The Pauline letter to the Colossians describes it as "the glorious riches of this mystery, which is Christ in you, the hope of glory." The timeless nondual awareness of Christ in us is the basis of the expectation that when our earthly existence ends, our true timeless nature will not end. Eternal life is now.

Jesus defines eternal life in this chapter. "This is eternal life, that they may know You, the only true God, and Jesus Christ whom You have sent." Eternal life is knowledge – knowledge of God and Christ. This is the foundation of gnostic Christianity. Gnosis is

the Greek word for knowledge, which is the word
used here in this passage.

Gnostic Christianity was not originally a heresy,
as it was declared to be in the second century. It was
part of the rich diversity of earliest Christianity.
Spiritual knowledge is the heart of the Gospel of
John. Jesus' definition of eternal life is knowledge.
Hindu spirituality calls it jnana, the way of
knowledge, one of the traditional Indian paths to
liberation.

This is not intellectual knowledge. This is not
doctrinal knowledge expressed in creeds and
expounded in theological tomes. This is spiritual
knowledge. This is firsthand knowing our true nature
and God's true nature, which is the divine name I
AM. This is unitive awareness in which there is no
division between knower and knowing and known.
All is one.

Jesus speaks of this knowledge in the second
section of the prayer. "I have revealed Your name to
the men whom You gave Me out of the world; they
were Yours and You gave them to Me, and they have
followed Your word." The Name that Jesus is
referring to is the eternal Name of the Divine, I AM.
The Word that he is referring to is the Eternal Logos,
his true identity. Logos is the Greek word used in
this verse.

Jesus goes on to pray for his disciples saying to
God, "All things that are Mine are Yours, and Yours
are Mine; and I have been glorified in them. I am no
longer going to be in the world; and yet they
themselves are in the world, and I am coming to You.
Holy Father, keep them in Your name, the name
which You have given Me, so that they may be one
just as We are." Jesus is saying that after his death,
his disciples will be in the Name – the I AM – and will
be one with him and God. This is nonduality.

The high point of the prayer comes in the third

section, where Jesus prays for those who become Christians through the testimony of the disciples. This is one of the greatest passages in the Bible, and one of the best descriptions of nonduality ever taught.

Jesus prays, "I am not asking on behalf of these alone, but also for those who believe in Me through their word, that they may all be one; just as You, Father, are in Me and I in You, that they also may be in Us, so that the world may believe that You sent Me. The glory which You have given Me I also have given to them, so that they may be one, just as We are one; I in them and You in Me, that they may be perfect in unity, so that the world may know that You sent Me, and You loved them, just as You loved Me."

Jesus is describing a perfect mystical unity of the believer and Christ and God. All are one, Jesus says. "You, Father, are in Me and I in You, that they also may be in Us." Jesus says that we are one with God in the same way that he is one with God. "So that they may be one, just as We are one; I in them and You in Me, that they may be perfect in unity."

Traditional Christian theology has a lot to say about Jesus' oneness with God. In fact it took most of the first four centuries and numerous church councils to work out the exact language of this oneness. The Nicene Creed uses the words "eternally begotten of the Father, God from God, Light from Light, true God from true God, begotten, not made, of one Being with the Father."

But traditional Christianity ignores the fact that Jesus says we have the same oneness with God. Jesus said he was giving us the same glory that he has. "The glory which You have given Me I also have given to them, so that they may be one, just as We are one; I in them and You in Me, that they may be perfected in unity." The phrases of the Nicene Creed that describe Jesus also describe us!

Of course voicing such a thing is heresy in traditional Christianity. Yet that is exactly what Jesus is saying. Today Christianity describes humans in terms of fallenness, sin, mortality, judgement and condemnation. Lots of negative language. At best it talks about us as creatures made in the image of God, but it never use the same words that are used for Christ. This is how far Christianity has "fallen" from the original gospel of Jesus.

We are in God, and God is in us. We are in Christ, and Christ is in us. We have the glory that Jesus has. We are one with the divine. Jesus calls it perfect unity. If that is not nonduality, I do not know what is! In the final words of the prayer Jesus describes this as divine love. He prays to God, "I have made Your name known to them, and will make it known, so that the love with which You loved Me may be in them, and I in them." This is the nondual gospel of Jesus proclaimed to us and through us. This is the unitive love that is being proclaimed in the Gospel of John. This is Christian nonduality.

NONDUALITY ON TRIAL

The Gospel of John is a proclamation that Jesus is the I AM, the nondual reality we call God. The structure of the Fourth Gospel emphasizes his divine identity with seven I AM statements. I AM – ego eimi in the Greek text – is a reference to the Divine Name revealed to Moses at the Burning Bush. In that story God calls this his eternal name. Every time Jesus uses those words he is proclaiming his true identity as Divine.

In the 18th and 19th chapters of the Gospel of John these words I AM take center stage. It is the account of the arrest and trial of Jesus. The opening scene on the Mount of Olives is a reenactment of the scene of Moses at the burning bush on Mount Sinai, when God spoke the words I AM.

Jesus traveled with his disciples from the city of Jerusalem, where they had just finished the Last Supper, across the Kidron Valley up the Mount of Olives and into the Garden of Gethsemane. The scene in Gethsemane takes place on the side of a mountain, just like the scene of Moses and the burning bush was on the side of Mount Sinai. A mob led by Judas Iscariot comes to Gethsemane carrying lanterns and torches. The torches echo the fire of the burning bush.

On Sinai God speaks and Moses falls to the ground before the great I AM. In the Garden of Gethsemane the crowd asks for Jesus, and he responds, "I AM." English translations often render this as "I am he," but the Greek text reads simply "Ego Eimi." I am. "Now then, when He said to them, "I AM," they drew back and fell to the ground." This response parallels Moses reaction to God, with Jesus playing the role of God. Jesus is pictured as the I AM.

The mob asks again, and Jesus responds again, "I AM." Three times Jesus is declared as the I AM to the people who came to arrest him. At first the apostle Peter tries to protect Jesus from the crowd with a sword, but Jesus tells him to put away his weapon. Then Peter follows the arresting crowd into the city and waits in the courtyard of the high Priest while Jesus is interrogated.

In the courtyard Peter is asked three times if he was a follower of Jesus, and three times Peter answers with the words "I am not." This is an intentional contrast between Jesus saying three times "I AM" and Peter saying three times "I am not."

There is a powerful spiritual message here. Jesus represents the spiritually realized person who knows he is the I AM. Peter represents the person who does not yet realize this. He says, "I am not." That is the predicament of every person. Either we know who we are or we do not. Peter is physically and spiritually pictured as in the darkness outside the high priest's house, not knowing who he is and unable to admit to himself or anyone who Jesus is.

On the other hand Jesus is inside the high priest's house and is the model of one who knows exactly who he is and says so clearly. Once again, this happens three times. First Jesus is brought to Annas, then the high priest Caiaphas, and then the

Roman governor Pilate. Not only is Jesus on trial, but his message of nonduality is on trial. The priests Annas and Caiaphas represent religious leaders who reject this teaching. Pilate plays the role of the seeker who is looking to determine the truth. Whether he will act upon the truth is another matter.

The religious leaders ask questions about Jesus' teaching, not to discover anything new but to find evidence against him. The high priest has already judged and condemned Jesus in his heart. Jesus responds to the questions accordingly. When the high priest asks Jesus about his teaching, he responds, "I have spoken openly to the world; I always taught in synagogues and in the temple area, where all the Jews congregate; and I said nothing in secret. Why are you asking Me? Ask those who have heard what I spoke to them. Look: these people know what I said." For that answer Jesus got a smack across the face. Jesus responded, "If I have spoken wrongly, testify of the wrong; but if rightly, why do you strike Me?"

The religious leaders were not interested in truth. They were interested in protecting their religious turf. The same is true today. Spiritual truth is not popular among religious people and leaders. Generally speaking most religions are only interested in hearing information that confirms their own version of Truth. They are not serious about hearing answers that might challenge their understanding. On the other hand, a true seeker asks tough questions – the harder, the better.

Recently I did an online interview with Luke Bricker on his podcast "The Spiritual Nomad." He has a quote on his web site. It reads, "Jesus was asked 183 questions. Jesus answered three. Jesus asked 307 questions. Leaders would do well to follow his lead. Let people ask questions. Don't try to answer all those questions. Ask lots of questions yourself."

It is important to question everything. Do not accept anything on religious authority alone. That is what I did a decade ago. I questioned everything about my life and faith. This was professionally dangerous and potentially costly because I was an ordained pastor. But I had gotten to the point in my life that I needed to know the truth, no matter what the cost. I could not live a lie. It was only when I was willing to honestly question all the answers given by Christianity that I was open to Truth.

I began to preach sermons that posed difficult questions instead of giving easy answers. Questions like: Is there a God? Is Christ the only way? Is the Bible true? These are fundamental questions that challenge the foundations of the Christian faith. They have to be investigated deeply and sincerely. Truth is found only through questions, not by accepting someone else's answers. Don't trust any religious authority that says they have the answers. Find the answers yourself.

Pilate is pictured as someone searching for answers. He asks Jesus whether he was the King of the Jews, and Jesus gives the wonderful answer that he is, but adds, "My kingdom is not of this world." Jesus says that his mission is to testify to truth, "For this purpose I have been born, and for this I have come into the world: to testify to the truth. Everyone who is of the truth listens to My voice." Pilate said to Him, "What is truth?"

Interpreters construe Pilate's response differently, but I think he was sincere. I understand Pilate as a seeker, and he saw something true in Jesus. That is why he declares Jesus innocent of all charges. In his words: "I find no grounds at all for charges in His case." He devises a way to release Jesus, but his accusers choose to release Barabbas instead. Pilate tries again to find some way to free Jesus, and so he interrogates him further. In the end Pilate chooses to be a pragmatic politician over a spiritual seeker. He chooses expediency over justice and truth. So he hands Jesus over to be flogged and crucified.

Jesus' trial is an example of religion in cahoots with political power to advance a social and political agenda. This is not only about Jesus on trial. His teachings were on trial as well. Specifically his nondual teachings were on trial. It is the same today. That is why you will not find the unitive approach taught in many churches. Christian nonduality downplays doctrine too much to be accepted as orthodox by most Christians.

Christian Nonduality is judged and condemned today, like Jesus was judged and condemned for his nondual teachings. So be it. We should not be surprised. Jesus spent the previous chapter warning us this would be the case. Nonduality represents a Reality – a Kingdom - that is not of this world, and for this reason the world does not understand or accept it.

This is a good thing. It frees us from the temptation to seek approval from establishment religion. It prevents us from accepting a teaching because it promises social or financial rewards. The nondual gospel is about dying to all of that. Dying to self. Dying to religious systems. Dying to power and influence. It is about dying to duality, so there might be resurrection to nonduality. This is where the cross and resurrection come in. This is what makes this Christian nonduality.

THE CROSS AND NONDUALITY

The symbol of the Christianity is the cross. It is also a powerful symbol of nonduality. But that is not how the death of Jesus is traditionally understood. In orthodox Christian thinking, the Cross is seen in transactional terms. It is thought that a transaction occurred on the Cross that objectively changed humankind's relationship to God. A transaction is by nature dualistic, defined as an exchange or interaction between two parties. There have to be two for there to be a transaction. If there is in reality not two – nondual – then there is no need for a transaction.

The usual dualistic interpretation of the cross is that Jesus' death was the price paid - or the sacrifice made - to reconcile sinful humans to a righteous God. It is seen as an atoning sacrifice, patterned after the sacrifice offered on the Jewish Day of Atonement. The strictest form of this theory of salvation is called substitutionary atonement, or penal substitutionary atonement. It is that idea that Jesus was punished (penalized) in the place of sinners (substitution), thus satisfying the demands of divine justice so God could forgive sin. The cross is understood as a legal transaction and is often described in terms taken from the courtroom. It is based on the assumption that there is a dualism that needs to be breached.

That model is not found in the gospels. If that had been the theology of the gospel writers then they would have had Jesus die on Yom Kippur, the Day of Atonement, the holiest day on the Jewish calendar. But they place it at the time of the Passover, which is not a temple sacrifice and has nothing to do with the forgiveness of sins or atonement for sin. If one believes in God as a Divine Monarch orchestrating Jesus' death from heaven, then it would have been easy enough for God to arrange for Jesus' death to happen on Yom Kippur. Then the meaning of his death would have been clear. But instead Jesus' death is connected to the Passover.

The Gospel of John emphasizes the connection with the Passover more than the other three gospels by changing the timing of Jesus' death slightly. In the first three gospels, the Last Supper is pictured as a Passover Meal, and the death of Jesus happens after the Passover. In John's Gospel Jesus dies before Passover - on the day of Preparation for the Passover - at the exact moment that the Passover lambs were slaughtered.

John was depicting Jesus as a Passover lamb. The Passover Lamb was not a sacrifice for sins. It was not offered in the tabernacle or the temple. The Passover was a family event celebrated in the home. According to the Exodus story the Passover was a deliverance from death. The blood of the lamb was not poured out on an altar as an atonement for sin. It was placed on the doorposts of Hebrew homes to protect them from the angel of death.

The cross is understood as a doorway with the blood of the Passover Lamb on it. It is a door from death to life. Jesus had previously called himself the Door and the Life. This is what John the Baptist meant when he called Jesus the Lamb of God. He even said, "Behold the Lamb of God who takes away the sin of the world." That has to be one of the most misinterpreted verses in the Bible. It does not mean that Jesus' death atones for sin. It means that it removes the concept of sin as an obstacle to God.

The Greek word used by John translated "takes away" is used more than a hundred times in the New Testament. It is never used in the sense of atoning for sin, paying the price for sin, or forgiving sin. This is a classic case of Christians reading theology into a text. This exact word is used four times in chapter 19 (that we are looking at now) where it is used to describe taking Jesus to the cross and taking his body from the cross. It is used four times in chapter 20 in reference to taking away the stone from a tomb entrance and removing the body of Jesus from the tomb. It is not about atoning or sacrificing or paying a penalty. It is removing a barrier to understanding our unity with God.

In the Gospel of John the death of Jesus is a symbol, not a transaction - a symbol based on the idea of the Passover Lamb. It represents new life through death. It symbolizes the death of the body and psyche, the death of the separate self. It is the sense of the individual self that separates us from God. Jesus taught that anyone who would be his disciple was to deny his or her self. Jesus taught us to die to self, to take up our cross and follow him. That is what the cross represents.

When we die to self we discover that we are one with God. Everyone finds this out when they physically die. When we physically die we return to what we were before birth. The good news is that we can discover this before we physically die by dying before we die. Jesus taught that it is only by losing our life that you gain life. Only by giving up one's separate mortal existence do we gain eternal life.

THE GOSPEL OF NONDUALITY

That is the symbolism of the Cross.

The Cross of Jesus stood between two other crosses. Two other men were crucified with Jesus, one on his right and one on his left. Jesus was in the center. The other gospels go so far as to picture one of the men as good and one as bad. One believes in Jesus and the other curses Jesus. This is classic dualism. This is the tree of the knowledge of good and evil. Good on one side of Jesus and evil on the other. Jesus is the Tree of Life in the middle. He represents nondual reality that reconciles the two opposites. Ephesians puts it this way: "For He Himself is our peace, who has made the two one and has torn down the dividing wall of hostility."

The symbol of the Cross is powerful even apart from Jesus, which is why it has a long history before it was adopted by Christianity. The vertical line unites heaven and earth. The horizontal line unites East and West. The two lines converge at the center, pointing to the center of our existence, which is identical to the reality of the universe. I prefer the Celtic cross over the Roman cross, not only because of my own Celtic heritage, but because it combines a cross with a circle, which is a symbol of wholeness, oneness or the Tao.

There is another wonderful symbol of nonduality in John's account of the death of Jesus. It is the seamless robe of Christ. When the Roman soldiers crucified Jesus they took off his tunic, which was a finely made seamless garment. It was probably a gift from one of his wealthier benefactors. The soldiers did not want to ruin the garment by tearing it into pieces, so they cast lots for it. John notes that this was in fulfillment of a prophecy about the Messiah in the Psalms.

There has been much speculation about this robe over the centuries. One account says that the robe was later recovered by the disciples. Centuries later the church cut it into pieces and divided it in order to protect it from theft or loss. That is ironic. What the Romans crucifers would not do, the church did. The church inherited the nondual message of Jesus and divided it into a message of duality. No less than six churches in Germany, France and Russia claim to possess the robe or fragments of it. There was even a film about the robe back in the 1950's, entitled "The Robe."

The Church Fathers saw the robe as a symbol for the unity of the church. I think it stands for the nonduality of reality. Jesus wore this robe – this nondual identity – in life. It symbolized his nature and his message. To communicate the same point, John's gospel says that no bone of Jesus' body was broken during this crucifixion. Death did not affect the unity of Jesus.

One more interesting detail. John's gospel says that when a soldier pierced his side to determine if he was dead, blood and water flowed from the wound. Although commentators focus on the physiological aspects of this, I think it is symbolic. The first letter of John talks about being born of God, saying, "This is the One who came by water and blood, Jesus Christ; not with the water only, but with the water and with the blood."

The gospel writer may have in mind Jesus' conversation with Nicodemus about being born anew, where they compare physical childbirth with all its bloodiness with spiritual rebirth. It is no accident that in the crucifixion story immediately after this is mentioned, Nicodemus suddenly appears on the scene to take away the body of Jesus for burial, setting the stage for the resurrection. I could go on, but the point is that in John's gospel the Cross of Jesus is deeply symbolic, pointing to the nondual reality of Jesus and his message.

NONDUAL EASTER

Easter is at the heart of Christian Nonduality. Two of the most famous Easter stories are in the 20th chapter of the Gospel of John. One is the familiar story of Mary Magdalene coming to the tomb of Jesus and finding the tomb already open and empty. She immediately informs two apostles, who come and confirm what she had discovered. Then there is the wonderful account of Magdalene lingering at the tomb, talking to angels and conversing with the groundskeeper, who turns out to be the risen Lord.

In this chapter there is also the equally famous story of Doubting Thomas. On Easter evening the risen Christ appeared to the apostles within a locked room, but Thomas was not present. When he hears about the visit, he refuses to believe that Jesus had risen. Eight days later, Jesus appears to the apostles again in the same room; this time Thomas is present. After being invited by the risen Christ to examine the wounds on his body, Thomas believes, declaring Jesus, "My Lord and my God." These resurrection stories – as well as those in the other three gospels – can be seen as a proclamation of nonduality.

First let's look at the empty tomb, which is the only common element found in all four gospels. The empty tomb is thought by scholars to be the earliest form of the Easter tradition. For example, in the original ending of the Gospel of Mark, which is widely accepted as the earliest of the four gospels, there are no appearances of the risen Christ. There is only the empty tomb. Historically speaking, it is widely accepted by biblical scholars that the earliest Easter message was the empty tomb. Only later did the stories of resurrection appearances begin to circulate.

What is the explanation for the empty tomb? There are suggestions embedded in the Easter stories. The most logical idea is that someone took the body. That is what we would think today if we came upon an empty tomb, which had been occupied earlier. This idea is voiced by Magdalene. She tells the disciples, "They have taken the Lord from the tomb, and we do not know where they have put Him." She repeats the idea to two angels that she sees at the tomb and also to the groundskeeper, for a total of three times.

There is no reason to doubt that the tomb of Jesus was empty on Easter morning. What does this mean? This is where we start talking in spiritual terms. The empty tomb is a symbol. It testifies that the true nature of Jesus was not his physical form. His true nature was not subject to death or decay, any more than our essential nature is.

Physical bodies are impermanent and therefore not real in an ultimate sense. Only that which does not change is ultimately real. In time our bodies dissolve into the elements from which they were made. Billions of graves lay empty today. Billions of people have died, and their bodies have returned to the elements from which they were formed. God says to Adam in Genesis, "You are dust and to dust you shall return." Our graves will be empty one day. For those of us who will be cremated and our ashes scattered, that day will be soon after death.

The empty tomb communicates our true nature. Emptiness is a symbol of nonduality. In Buddhism it is called the void or Sunyata. The empty tomb stories proclaim that Jesus returned to the Emptiness which is his true nature. He became after death what he was before birth. So do we. We are the emptiness. In the Tao Te Ching, the Tao is described as empty space. It is represented by a circle that looks like the mouth of an empty tomb.

In the Old Testament God is said to occupy the empty space between the wings of the cherubim above the Ark of the Covenant in the Holy of Holies. God is emptiness. To say that God is Spirit is to say the same thing – that God is empty of form. Spirit is non material, nonphysical, literally no thing. This is the true nature of Christ and our true nature.

The resurrection appearances also teach us about the nature of Christ. First there is the appearance of Jesus to Magdalene at the Garden Tomb. The first element of this resurrection story is that Mary did not recognize Christ. She thought he was the gardener. All sorts of reasons for this mistaken identity are offered by preachers. The simplest explanation is that the risen Lord did not look like Jesus.

This is a theme in nearly all the resurrection stories. On almost every occasion the disciples did not recognize the risen Christ. They are always wondering who this stranger is. We see this in Chapter 21 when some disciples had breakfast with Jesus on the beach. We see it in the much loved Emmaus Road story. Two disciples walked for miles with Jesus on the Emmaus Road without recognizing him.

The message is clear. Christ comes incognito. It reminds me of the verse in the Letter to the Hebrews that says, "Do not neglect to show hospitality to strangers, for thereby some have entertained angels unawares." It reminds me of the parable where Jesus comes in the form of the poor, hungry, thirsty, sick, homeless and imprisoned; people do not recognize him. People will say, "When did we see you hungry or thirsty, or as a stranger, or naked, or sick, or in prison, and take care of You?' Then He will answer them, 'Truly I say to you, Jesus says, "As you have done to the least of these my brothers, you have done to me."

The Risen Christ comes in every man and women. Evangelicals are expecting the Second Coming of Christ any day now. They are expecting him to fly down physically from the sky like Superman returning from Krypton. The truth is that Christ is here now, but he is not recognized by his disciples. There is no room in the inn – again. He comes in the form of the immigrant at our borders. He comes in the gay youth who is bullied. He comes in the unarmed black youth shot in the street. Easter is about recognizing the risen Christ in those we would not think of as Christ. Christ is with us always, even as he said, if we have eyes to see.

Another important element of John's resurrection stories is the physicality of the appearances. The risen Christ is described not as a ghost or a spirit, but as flesh and blood. Magdalene is told by Jesus not to hold onto him. Thomas is invited to examine the wounds of the risen Christ. The risen Christ eats food with the disciples. In the Gospel of Luke the risen Christ says, "See my hands and my feet, that it is I myself. Touch me, and see. For a spirit does not have flesh and bones as you see that I have." In John's gospel the risen Lord has physical form, but it is not a normal physical form. He is able to miraculously appear within locked rooms, for example, but he is physical nonetheless.

Why this emphasis on the physicality of the risen

Christ? It is so that we will recognize the risen Christ in the physical form of people around us. This is a call to serve Christ by meeting people's physical needs. Equally important is the idea that a physical body is no barrier to spiritual realization. We don't have to become disembodied spirits to enter the Kingdom of God. We can know nondual reality before death.

The physicality of the resurrection is no problem in Christian Nonduality because there is no distinction between the physical and the spiritual. They are one. When people ask me if the resurrection of Jesus was physical or spiritual, I respond that it is nondual. Physical and spiritual are one.

There is a parallel in physics, which says there is no essential difference between matter and energy. I am no Einstein, but as I understand it, matter is energy in a different form. Matter (as mass) and energy can be converted into each other according to that famous equation $E=mc^2$. Mass can be converted to energy and energy to mass. It is no miracle. I watch it happen every time I put a log into my woodstove. Wood turns to energy and heats my home. It is a living example of nonduality. Physical is spiritual and vice versa. The two are one.

The resurrection points to the reality that the physical Christ is the spiritual Christ. There is no essential difference between the two. This reality is what Christianity calls the Holy Spirit, who is said to dwell within us. In the Gospel of John the giving of the Holy Spirit happens as part of the Easter story. On the evening of Easter day the risen Christ appears suddenly within locked doors to his disciples and gives them the Holy Spirit.

"Jesus came and stood in their midst, and said to them, "Peace be to you." And when He had said this, He showed them both His hands and His side. The disciples then rejoiced when they saw the Lord. So

Jesus said to them again, "Peace be to you; just as the Father has sent Me, I also send you." And when He had said this, He breathed on them and said to them, "Receive the Holy Spirit."

The Gospel of Luke and Acts places the receiving of the Holy Spirit weeks later on the Day of Pentecost, ten days after Jesus' ascension. But in John's Gospel it is part of the resurrection story of Easter Sunday. It is placed on Easter to communicate the truth that the Holy Spirit is the Spirit of Christ. The risen Christ shares his spirit, his essential nature with us. This Holy Spirit can also be called Self-Realization or Christ Consciousness.

The risen Christ is in us, "Christ in us the hope of glory." I believe Christ is risen because I know this reality in everyday life. I see Christ in everything – in every person and creature and in every part of God's creation, including myself. As Paul says, "It is no longer I who live but Christ who lives in me." That is the truth of the resurrection of Jesus Christ. Christ is risen. He is risen indeed.

RESURRECTION REPRISED

The final chapter of the Gospel of John is actually a postscript. The verses at the end of chapter 20 are clearly intended to be the conclusion of the book. Chapter 21 was added at a later date. At some time after the Gospel was written, a final editor decided to attach one final resurrection scene to the gospel.

This extra chapter was added because of the death of the apostle John. John was the leader of the spiritual community in Ephesus out of which this gospel came. He was also the last surviving member of the original twelve apostles, the final physical link to the historical Jesus. During his later life John had become the de facto head of the whole church, so his death was a significant event.

Furthermore there was a rumor circulating in the early church that Jesus had prophesied that the apostle John would not die before the Kingdom of God came to earth. People were expecting the end of the world soon. Then John died and nothing changed, leaving the church wondering what went wrong. Was Jesus mistaken? It was a crisis of faith for many Christians. This chapter was added to address this crisis. We see this issue referred to in this conversation between Peter and Jesus.

"Peter turned around and saw the disciple whom Jesus loved following them—the one who also had leaned back on His chest at the supper and said, "Lord, who is the one who is betraying You?" So Peter, upon seeing him, said to Jesus, "Lord, and what about this man?" Jesus said to him, "If I want him to remain until I come, what is that to you? You follow Me!" Therefore this account went out among the brothers, that that disciple would not die; yet Jesus did not say to him that he would not die, but only, "If I want him to remain until I come, what is that to you?"

This crisis raised the issue of the nature of the Second Coming. The belief in an imminent physical return of Jesus was based on an interpretation of Jesus' words spoken in the Olivet Discourse in the synoptic gospels, where he said, "Truly I say to you, there are some of those who are standing here who will not taste death until they see the Son of Man coming in His kingdom." Luke's version says, "There are some standing here who will not taste death until they see the kingdom of God."

There developed a popular belief that this referred to the return of Jesus to earth. Many evangelicals and fundamentalists still believe in an imminent physical Second Coming of Jesus. If that is what Jesus meant, then Jesus was wrong. That whole generation died and many generations after that, and still there has been no physical Second Coming of Jesus. That is a problem for literalists then and now.

But that is not what Jesus meant. Jesus meant that his generation would not die before some of those standing there would see the Kingdom of God within us and all around us. Jesus said, "The Kingdom of God is within you." That is what Jesus was talking about in his conversation with Nicodemus. Jesus said to him, "Unless one is born again, he cannot see the Kingdom of God." Jesus was talking about a spiritual awakening not a Second Coming. That is what it means to see the Kingdom of God. That is what it means to enter the Kingdom of God.

The death of the last apostle also meant a change in leadership in the wider church. With John gone, who would the church look to for spiritual guidance? The leadership of the church determines the teaching of the church. A change in leadership means a change in theology. The leadership eventually decided to reject the nondual teachings and retain what is known as the "proto-orthodox" position, which became traditional Christianity. That is why there are so few nondual teachings in the New Testament today.

At the end of the first century there was a rivalry between the Church in Ephesus – where John's spiritual community was located - and the Church of Rome, where Peter was the first bishop. The 21st chapter was added to address this question of leadership.

In this chapter there is a discussion between Jesus and Peter about tending his sheep, which is ecclesiastical jargon for being a pastoral leader. Jesus asked Peter three times if he loved him. Peter responded three times that he did love him. Jesus replied by instructing Peter three times to tend his sheep or feed his sheep. This means to be the shepherd, the pastor of the church.

As every preacher knows, the key to understanding this passage is found in the Greek words for love. Both Jesus and Peter speak of love in the text, but they use different Greek words with very different meanings. Jesus uses the word agape – divine unconditional love. Jesus asks Peter twice if he loves him with agape love - divine unconditional love. Peter responds saying he loves Jesus, but uses the word philia, which means human emotional love.

The third time Jesus asks if Peter loves him with this philia love. Jesus calls into question if Peter has human love for Jesus, much less divine love.

The Gospel of John calls into question the love of Peter for Jesus and hence the right of Peter (and his successors in Rome) to be the leader of the church. John is pictured as one who loves and is loved with divine love. Throughout the Gospel of John, John is repeatedly called the beloved apostle. The word beloved is a form of the word agape. John represents divine love. Peter does not even measure up to the standard of human love. In other words, this story was meant to undermine the leadership of Peter and therefore the bishop of Rome.

The seemingly innocuous fishing story that opens the chapter does the same thing, but in a more subtle manner. Chapter 21 begins with seven apostles going on a fishing trip to the Sea of Galilee. Peter is pictured as the leader of the expedition. He declared he was going fishing, and six of the apostles (about half, which is meant to show how divided the church was) decided to follow him. They spent all night fishing, but under Peter's leadership they caught nothing. Peter's leadership failed. He could not even catch fish. How could he possibly lead the church? The fishing is pictured as happening at night, a time of darkness. Darkness in John's gospel is always symbolic as well as physical.

Then dawn comes. The risen Christ arrives on the scene and points out where the fish are located. All they had to do is try fishing on the other side of the boat! Only then do they catch anything. They haul in 153 fish. An exact number like 153 this is very rare in the gospels. Numbers are always rounded off. For example earlier John does not say that Jesus fed 5087 people with a few loaves and fishes, but rounds it off to five thousand. Here it says that the disciples netted exactly 153 fish. Our attention is being drawn to this number and its meaning.

We see the same use of symbolic numbers in the Book of Revelation, which is also part of the Johannine corpus. Revelation was said to be written by the apostle John. It certainly came out of this same spiritual community in Ephesus. In the Revelation of John the number 666 was symbolic for the name of the Beast. In Greek and Latin every letter had a numerical equivalent. The name of Caesar Nero – the villain of Revelation - added up to 666. In the Gospel of John, the name Magdalene adds up to 153.

We have already seen the prominence of Mary Magdalene in this gospel. She was the first to see the risen Lord. She was the first to proclaim the message of the risen Lord to the apostles. For that reason she is often called the "apostle to the apostles." Her name is hidden in this story of Jesus appearing to seven disciples at the Sea of Galilee.

In this fish story Jesus was symbolically declaring Mary Magdalene to be the true spiritual leader of the church! In telling this tale, the final editor of the Gospel of John was thumbing his nose at the apostle Peter and the bishops of Rome. Peter and his male successors may claim to be the leaders of the Church, but they are incompetent. They cannot even catch fish. How could they possibly fulfill Jesus' commission to be "fishers of men?" Mary Magdalene was more a leader than Peter.

We know from the non-canonical Christian writings known as the Nag Hammadi library, discovered in Egypt in 1945, that there was a strong movement in the early church that believed that Mary Magdalene was the rightful heir of Jesus. There are many books in that collection that confirm that – books such as the Dialogue of the Savior, the Gospel of Philip, and the Sophia of Jesus Christ. The Gospel of Mary was written from her perspective. In the

Gospel of Mary, the Gospel of Thomas and the Pistis Sophia (meaning the Wisdom of Faith), we see Peter opposing the leadership of Mary. These books show us that that there was a struggle for leadership going on between men and women in the early church.

The Nag Hammadi scrolls, many of which are nondual in nature, reveal to us that there was a strong mystical tradition in early Christianity that was later suppressed by the Church. Those spiritual communities were often led by women in the tradition of Magdalene. That is why Mary Magdalene plays such a prominent roles in so many of these writings. They were the true heirs of the nondual gospel of Jesus Christ. The Gospel of John is affirming that tradition.

Of course historically women lost the battle for leadership in the church. In the process the nondual gospel lost out to the dualistic gospel, and the nondual books were banned. Most copies of these early gospels and epistles were destroyed, but some were hidden. These we have in the New Testament apocrypha, including the Nag Hammadi scrolls.

Women leadership was controversial even at the turn of the second century at the time when the Gospel of John was finalized. This is why Magdalene's name had to be hidden in a symbolic number in John's gospel. This chapter of John never would have made it into the Bible if her leadership had been more clearly affirmed. Only by the grace of God did this symbolic reference to Mary sneak past the censors.

In this context of leadership, the Gospel of John proclaims the primacy of love. John shows that Peter did not the love that Jesus wanted. This was confirmed by the threefold profession of Peter that he loved Jesus, but not in a nondual way of identification, as the beloved disciple loved Jesus. In the Gospel of Mary, part of the Nag Hammadi library,

Mary Magdalene is often referred to as being loved by Jesus and loving Jesus more than the others.

The Gospel of John calls us to a love that transcends dualism. Nondual love is not a relationship but a union with the Beloved. It is a union so strong that one's own identity recedes into the background. That is why John never refers to himself by name in this gospel. He is always referred to as the Beloved Disciple. His individual sense of identity had dissolved in the love of Christ. That is nondual love in which two become one. Jesus invites us to enter into oneness. That is the message of the Gospel of John.

ABOUT THE AUTHOR

Marshall Davis is an ordained American Baptist minister who has served American Baptist and Southern Baptist churches in New Hampshire, Massachusetts, Pennsylvania, Illinois and Kentucky during his forty year ministry as a pastor.

He holds a Bachelor of Arts degree in Religion from Denison University, as well as Master of Divinity and Doctor of Ministry degrees from the Southern Baptist Theological Seminary, Louisville, Kentucky. He has done sabbatical studies at the Tantur Ecumenical Institute for Theological Research in Jerusalem, Israel; Regent's Park College of Oxford University, Oxford, England; and the Shalem Institute for Spiritual Formation in Washington. D.C.

He has a podcast entitled "The Tao of Christ," a YouTube Channel called "Christian Nonduality" and a blog entitled "Spiritual Reflections." He is the author of several books. Links to these resources can be found at MarshallDavis.us or PastorDavis.com.

Having retired from fulltime pastoral ministry in 2016, nowadays he spends most days with his wife at their 18th century home in a small village in the White Mountains of New Hampshire. There he enjoys the mountains and lakes, vegetable gardening, walking, playing backgammon and cribbage, and watching his grandchildren grow. He writes nearly every day and preaches occasionally at nearby churches.

Other Books by Marshall Davis

Experiencing God Directly: The Way of Christian Nonduality

The Tao of Christ: A Christian Version of the Tao Te Ching

Living Presence: A Guide to Everyday Awareness of God

The Practice of the Presence of God in Modern English by Brother Lawrence, translated by Marshall Davis

Christianity Without Beliefs

Thank God for Atheists: What Christians Can Learn from the New Atheism

The Seeker's Journey: A Contemporary Retelling of Pilgrim's Progress

What Your Pastor Won't Tell You (But I Can Because I'm Retired)

Understanding Revelation

The Evolution of Easter: How the Historical Jesus Became the Risen Christ

The Parables of Jesus: American Paraphrase Version

More Than a Purpose: An Evangelical Response to Rick Warren and the Megachurch Movement

The Baptist Church Covenant: Its History and Meaning

A People Called Baptist: An Introduction to Baptist History & Heritage

Made in the USA
Las Vegas, NV
14 August 2023

76087396R00081